Age of the Offered Hand

The Centre for the Study of Democracy's (CSD) Library of Political Leadership

One of the first questions to ask about any leader is what are his or her priorities and do they run with or against the grain of history? An essential way of determining this is to research the public record and then compare dreams versus accomplishments. It is the public record of measured words that remains the most reliable barometer of either consistency or change in one's purpose. As Lord Acton wrote to the contributors to the Cambridge Modern History Project, "archives are meant to be explored". And because the written word is the key to describing ruling currents and interpreting sovereign forces, "we must provide a copious, accurate, and well-digested catalogue of authorities". To understand a public figure it is necessary to start with what he or she said and wrote. This is the third volume in the CSD's Library of Political Leadership, an occasional series of collections of the public addresses of Canadian Prime Ministers, Premiers, opposition politicians and significant foreign leaders in the Canadian context.

Thomas S. Axworthy
Chair, Centre for the Study of Democracy
Library of Political Leadership Series General Editor

Age of the Offered Hand

The Cross-Border Partnership Between
President George H.W. Bush and Prime Minister Brian Mulroney,
A Documentary History

Introductions by
DEREK H. BURNEY AND THE HON. ROBERT A. MOSBACHER, SR.

Edited by
JAMES MCGRATH AND ARTHUR MILNES

Volume III in the Queen's Centre for the Study of Democracy
Library of Political Leadership Occasional Series
Thomas S. Axworthy, Series General Editor
School of Policy Studies, Queen's University
McGill-Queen's University Press
Montreal & Kingston • London • Ithaca

SCHOOL OF
Policy Studies

Publications Unit
Policy Studies Building
138 Union Street
Kingston, ON, Canada
K7L 3N6
www.queensu.ca/sps/

Library and Archives Canada Cataloguing in Publication

Age of the offered hand : the cross-border partnership between President George H.W. Bush and Prime Minister Brian Mulroney, a documentary history / introductions by Derek H. Burney and Robert A. Mosbacher, Sr. ; edited by James McGrath and Arther Milnes.

(Library of political leadership occasional series ; v. 3)
Published for the Centre for the Study of Democracy, School of Policy
    Studies, Queen's University.
Includes speeches and correspondence of George H.W. Bush and Brian
    Mulroney.
ISBN 978-1-55339-233-0 (bound).--ISBN 978-1-55339-232-3 (pbk.)

1. Free trade--Canada--History--Sources. 2. Free trade--United States--History--Sources. 3. Bush, George W. (George Walker), 1946-. 4. Mulroney, Brian, 1939-. 5. Canada--Commerce--History--20th century--Sources. 6. United States--Commerce--History--20th century--Sources. I. Bush, George W. (George Walker), 1946- II. Mulroney, Brian, 1939- III. McGrath, James Gerald, 1967- IV. Milnes, Arthur, 1966- V. Queen's University (Kingston, Ont.). Centre for the Study of Democracy VI. Series: Library of political leadership series ; v. 3

HF1746.A345 2009 382'.971073 C2009-903563-4

Table of Contents

Acknowledgements

Our first acknowledgement is to both President Bush and the Right Honourable Mr. Mulroney, and their families, for the trust they have shown both editors over the years. McGrath first worked at the Bush White House starting in 1991, and still works closely with the president. Milnes served as Mr. Mulroney's research assistant for five years, 2003 to 2008, on the Mulroney *Memoirs*. Both the president and the former prime minister allowed McGrath and Milnes to fully cooperate during those years, and the phone lines and email links between Houston, Texas (McGrath) and Kingston, Ontario (Milnes) were well used.

This book would not have been published without the generous financial backing of a variety of people. Former Mulroney cabinet ministers the Hon. Barbara McDougall and the Hon. Michael Wilson (now Canada's Ambassador to the United States) were the first to offer their support. Mr. Peter Munk and Anthony S. Fell, both of Toronto, were also more than generous with their donations to defray the costs of publishing this volume. Finally, a number of Mr. Mulroney's classmates from St. Francis Xavier University also eagerly provided donations. The editors would like to recognize Mr. Justice James Chadwick of Ottawa, Terry McCann, former Mayor of Pembroke, Mr. Justice Cameron McCarthur of Ottawa, and James Nasso of Scarborough.

At Queen's University, Thomas S. Axworthy, chair of the Centre for the Study of Democracy, merits both personal and professional thanks from Milnes for his support of this project. Senator Hugh Segal, a proud Kingstonian and Queen's man (who served as Chief of Staff to Prime Minister Mulroney), and his wife Donna, have, like Dr. Axworthy, extended professional and personal courtesies and support for which Milnes and his wife are profoundly grateful. Dr. Arthur Sweetman, former director of the School of Policy Studies recognized the value of this examination of the bilateral cooperation between an American president and a Canadian prime minister, in this context and in others. Without his support this book would not have been possible. At the School of Policy Studies publishing unit, Mark Howes and his team performed the sort of superb work on this volume that they are known for in academic and publishing circles. Copy editor Anne Holley-Hime has earned thanks as well. Also in Kingston, retired politician, family doctor and community leader, Dr. Hans Westenberg, merits thanks from Milnes for his support. In Toronto, lawyer Samuel Wakim, Q.C., provided crucial support for this book for which the editors are grateful.

W.H. Milnes, a Scarborough history teacher, died suddenly on 18 August 2006. He passed on to his son a special passion for Canadian and

American history, particularly in politics and the field of prime ministers and presidents. He would be very proud of this book, as he was of his son's role as an assistant to Canada's former prime minister. Unfortunately, he did not live to see his family name graciously mentioned by Mr. Mulroney in *Memoirs*. Milnes would like to dedicate his work on this volume to a father and friend who inspired his son's love and joy of history at home, just as he did for countless students in Scarborough classrooms, and through the famous R.H. King Collegiate History Club, during his career.

McGrath would similarly like to dedicate this work to his parents, Anne and James, who have bestowed on him, respectively, a wonder of writing and a sense of service to country. He also would like to salute his stepfather, Fred Favo, for his decades of loyal service to his fellow citizens as a public servant in Oakmont, Pennsylvania.

Lastly, both editors would like to extend their thanks to Jean Becker, President George H.W. Bush's veteran chief of staff and former First Lady Barbara P. Bush.

James McGrath and Arthur Milnes

Editors' Note

> I was a big believer then, and still am, that personal diplomacy can be
> very useful and productive. George H.W. Bush, October 2007

President Bush wrote these reflective words in his 2007 preface to the *China Diary of George H.W. Bush: The Making of a Global President*.[1] They could have been written by Canada's 18th Prime Minister, Brian Mulroney, as well.

Both leaders, Bush in the United States as president from 1989 to 1993, and Mulroney as prime minister of Canada from 1984–1993, not only practiced this style of diplomacy—they demonstrated its value in the broadest possible global context.

Their partnership, as this collection aims to establish, offers a positive historic model for cooperation between our two nations. It is also being published to assist marking the 20th anniversary of the great free trade debate election in Canada. On 21 November 1988, Mulroney's Progressive Conservatives were returned to majority power by Canadians after running on the platform of free trade with the United States. Mulroney's success came after the most engaging and passionate national debate in modern Canadian history. Voter participation in Canada for that election stood at almost 76 percent, a figure not seen since. Free trade with the United States was an issue that saw one of Canada's greatest prime ministers, Sir Wilfrid Laurier, defeated in 1911 when espousing the cause. A generation later, Mackenzie King, prime minister for 22 years, backed down in fear at the thought of facing Canadians after securing a free trade deal, one that was surely within his grasp.

It was Brian Mulroney, of all Canada's prime ministers, who was finally able to embrace free trade—and win.

In the United States, November 2008 also marked the 20th anniversary of Bush's election as president. After playing a key role in the successful negotiation of the Free Trade Agreement between Canada and the United States as vice president, Bush and his team led by Secretary of Commerce Robert A. Mosbacher, Sr., Secretary of State James A.Baker III, and United States Trade Representative (USTR) head Carla Hills led the expansion of the FTA to the North American Free Trade Agreement (NAFTA) with Mexico, creating a continental partnership unheard of until then.

---

1   Bush, George H.W. (2008). *China Diary of George H.W. Bush The Making of a Global President*, ed. Jeffrey A. Engel. Princeton: Princeton University Press.

At the Centre for the Study of Democracy at Queen's University, (CSD), chair Dr. Thomas S. Axworthy made the 20th anniversary of the Canada–US free trade election, examining NAFTA and highlighting the overall issue of Canada–US relations, a high priority. This book is testimony to these valuable efforts on Dr. Axworthy's part, and we salute him for this personal commitment and that of the CSD. It is also thanks to him and the CSD that the major public addresses of Canada's 17th prime minister, the Right Honourable John N. Turner, Mulroney's main opponent in the historic 1988 election who passionately opposed the FTA, were published this past fall.

Age of the Offered Hand and *Politics of Purpose 40th Anniversary Edition* are both volumes in the CSD's new Library of Political Leadership, an occasional series of books that will ensure that the public addresses and writings of Canadian political leaders, prime ministers, premiers, opposition leaders and significant foreign leaders will be available to future students.

The November 1988 election in Canada was a seminal moment for Canadians (and Americans) and both these CSD volumes, it is hoped, will contribute to the understanding of the FTA, help us mark this noteworthy anniversary, and assist citizens on both sides of the border in gaining a broader understanding of Canadian-American relations.

George Herbert Walker Bush entered the White House having already demonstrated an intimate knowledge of, and interest in, Canada–US relations, unparalleled in scope and not seen since the days of Franklin Roosevelt. By the time he took the oath of office on a cold Washington day in January 1989, he had already played a crucial role in the successful negotiation of the Canada–US Free Trade Agreement; came to Ottawa at short notice to receive "an earful" (his words) on the acid rain issue from an angry Mulroney; and sat with seven members of the Canadian cabinet for an unprecedented meeting in 1986.

As president, Bush sent a clear signal concerning the importance of the cross-border relationship by making sure Canada was the site of his first foreign visit, less than a month after his swearing in. The night before his arrival in Ottawa, he told a joint session of Congress:

> If we're to protect our future, we need a new attitude about the environment. I will send you shortly legislation for a new, more effective Clean Air Act. It will include a plan to reduce by a certain date the emissions which cause acid rain, because the time for study alone had passed, and the time for action is now. We must make use of clean coal. My budget contains full funding, on schedule, for the clean-coal technology agreement that we've made with Canada. We've made that agreement with Canada, and we intend to honour that agreement.

This commitment, announced publicly to the Congress and the world, was crucial in cementing the coming cross-border partnership. "I had waited almost five years for an American president to speak the words he did that night," Mulroney—who made the fight against acid rain a personal prime ministerial priority—later wrote.[2]

Having established a solid foundation of goodwill, their partnership quickly thrived. The president valued the advice of his friend in Ottawa, Mulroney, so much so that the prime minister played a key role, like none had before, as the Cold War ended.

When the Berlin Wall "fell" in November 1989, in fact, it was Mulroney who delivered, in person, private messages from the American president to Mikhail Gorbachev at the Kremlin.[3] As the US president prepared for his first face-to-face summit with his Soviet counterpart off Malta the following month, he turned to Mulroney for a personal briefing about Gorbachev, held at the White House. For his part, Mulroney repaid this trust, sharing with the president of the United States and his senior foreign policy advisors his impressions of Gorbachev, which he had written only days before, in his personal diary.

German Chancellor Helmut Kohl later honoured a select group of statesman for their efforts to spearhead Central and East Europe's peaceful transition away from Soviet influence when the longstanding dream of German re-unification became a reality. "Looking back, I must name three people who really helped us," Kohl told a committee of the German Reichstag. "I am referring only to heads of state and government... There was George Bush, who did not hesitate for one minute when it came to German unity... There was Brian Mulroney. And there was Mikhail Gorbachev."[4]

The US–Canada friendship was as strong as it was from 1989 to 1993 because the personal friendship between their leaders was genuine. In fact, by the summer of 1989, their families had begun a tradition that continues to this day: visiting together at the Bush family retreat at Kennebunkport, Maine. During the summer of 1990, it should be noted, the world was a very unstable place. Saddam Hussein invaded Kuwait; and Bush, assisted by Mulroney, collaborated that summer to start forging the UN-sponsored coalition that eventually liberated Kuwait.

For example, at a White House meeting just hours after Hussein's tanks rolled into Kuwait, Bush sought Mulroney's advice in person at an un-scheduled meeting. As leader of the Western Alliance, Bush faced a difficult task in dealing with Hussein's aggression. On Mulroney's suggestion, Bush arranged a personal and consultative telephone call with French President

---

2   Mulroney, Brian. (2007). *Memoirs*. Toronto: McClelland and Stewart. pp 649–650.

3   Mulroney, see *Memoirs*, 699.

4   Mulroney, see *Memoirs*, 725.

XII

François Mitterrand to prove that America, through the United Nations, sought to be collaborative.

Mulroney also made it clear that Canada could not participate unless actions in response to Hussein took place with UN approval. On other occasions, Bush and Mulroney consulted endlessly on the telephone, compared notes on fellow world leaders, worked together to assemble the Coalition—including moderate Arab countries—that removed Hussein from Kuwait. Not since the era of Franklin Roosevelt and Mackenzie King has a partnership at this level been put into play to serve not only Canada and the United States, but the UN, NATO and countless other world forums.

Space does not permit us, as editors, to fully explore in this note the full extent of the Bush-Mulroney partnership. Our intention is to allow readers to form their own conclusions based on the joint public statements and appearances by the two leaders from 1989 to 1993 and on into political retirement. The George H.W. Bush Presidential Library at College Station, Texas, through its excellent website and staff, played a key role in our assembling the primary material for this volume, including pictures. Additional speeches were graciously provided to us by Mr. Mulroney, through his loyal and effective assistant Francine Collins. Photos as well came, with Mr. Mulroney's permission, from Library and Archives Canada in Ottawa.

While the personal archival collections of the 41st president and the 18th prime minister are not yet open fully to researchers, both men made extensive use of their archival records in preparing publications now on the public record. We recommend *A World Transformed: The Collapse of the Soviet Empire, The Unification of Germany, Tiananmen Square, The Gulf War* and the Mulroney *Memoirs* for those who wish to explore the Bush-Mulroney relationship further.[5]

We have included speeches, press coverage transcripts, some correspondence and writings in chronological fashion. These show their joint work in various subjects and policy areas: 1) The Environment; 2) Trade Liberalization; 3) Cold War; 4) The Gulf War; 5) Personal Relations; and 6) Political Retirement.

We have done minor editing. In terms of joint press conferences, we edited out questions that distracted from the flow of Canadian-American relations and the Bush-Mulroney partnership. An example in this area would be the questions some members of the press fired at the president concerning the fictitious television character Murphy Brown at the White House in 1992.

James McGrath and Arthur Milnes

5   Bush, George and Brent Scowcroft. (1998). *A World Transformed: The Collapse of the Soviet Empire, The Unification of Germany, Tiananmen Square, The Gulf War.* New York: Alfred A. Knopf. Also see Mulroney Brian. (2008) *Memoirs.* Toronto: McClelland and Stewart.

Introduction

DEREK H. BURNEY

The close personal relationship between President George H.W. Bush and Prime Minister Brian Mulroney is the exception to Lord Palmerston's adage that "nations have no permanent friends or allies, they only have permanent interests." The unique association between these two North American leaders embraced both friendship and interests and generated achievements for Canada and the United States to a level seldom, if ever, surpassed. The friendship extended well beyond issues of mutual interest or concern to the two leaders involving, as well, joint family vacations and warm celebrations of intimate family events.

Brian Mulroney initiated contact when George Bush served as Ronald Reagan's vice president and made a point of meeting Mr. Bush during each of his visits to Washington. On one memorable occasion, when the vice president reciprocated with a meeting in Ottawa, he received what he publicly characterized as "an earful" of complaint from the prime minister about Washington's inattention to key bilateral issues, notably free trade and acid rain. The frank exchange epitomized the growing friendship and, eventually, historic agreements were concluded on both issues. Negotiations for each were successful essentially because of leadership and persistence from the top in both capitals.

One summer in Kennebunkport, President Bush received a different kind of earful—an errant fish hook. The Canadian media were convinced that the culprit was their prime minister, but Jeb Bush volunteered gamely, possibly diplomatically, that he was responsible, thus enabling bilateral issues to survive this fish (fishy?) incident.

Brian Mulroney had an unusual knowledge of America, especially American politics. George Bush, as a frequent resident of Maine, was well-attuned to Canadian concerns and proclivities. The combination was impressive. They were very much at ease discussing bilateral or global concerns and were relentless in prodding constructive action. Their terms of office coincided with dramatic global change—the fall of the Berlin Wall, the collapse of the Soviet Union, the end of apartheid in South Africa, the UN-endorsed Gulf War and the conclusion of the NAFTA negotiations. Each of these events prompted an unprecedented series of exchanges and meetings between the two leaders, reviewing tactics and strategies as well as broader G-7 consultations. The candour and value of these discussions reflected a unique degree of mutual trust and confidence, and a positive tone that permeated both governments. The results were tangible and beneficial. The "permanent interests" of both countries were significantly enhanced. The personal friendship endures and transcends any normal definition of "good relations."

From different backgrounds and from different positions of power in world affairs, these two leaders forged a bond of true friendship that stands as a hallmark for others to emulate. This book is a tribute to that friendship and to the achievements it made possible.

On a personal note, as a proud graduate of Queen's University, where I earned my Bachelor of Arts in 1962 and Masters of Arts in 1964—and was able, while in Kingston, to attend campaign events featuring two political giants of that time, Prime Ministers Lester B. Pearson and John Diefenbaker—I am pleased my *alma mater*, through the Queen's University Centre for the Study of Democracy and under the leadership of Dr. Thomas S. Axworthy, has worked so hard to produce this volume. Dr. Axworthy's foresight in founding the CSD's Library of Political Leadership series of occasional publications will be commended and of real service to all those who seek a greater understanding of political leadership and public policy.

Hon. Robert A. Mosbacher, Sr.

In November 2004, at the dedication of the William Jefferson Clinton Presidential Library in Little Rock, Arkansas, President Jimmy Carter offered a fairly robust—and memorable—assessment of a former political adversary, George Herbert Walker Bush, when he observed that the 41st president of the United States had amassed "a career of public service to this country that is almost unmatched in history."

It was memorable for the simple reason that I don't always find myself in agreement with President Carter's views.

It was robust because the varied achievements President Carter cited that day—war hero, pioneering businessman, congressman, ambassador to the United Nations and China, director of Central Intelligence, vice president and finally, commander-in-chief—were reminiscent of a by-gone era of American statesmen.

Yet, even if he did enter office with a breadth of experience that harkened back to the days of our country's founders, George Bush also had the self-awareness to "know what he didn't know"—and the self-confidence to surround himself with a team of strong, and strong-willed, advisors. Names like Baker, Powell, Scowcroft, Cheney—all forceful people, all formidable personalities. None doubted who was in charge, however.

The president was equally deft when it came to interacting with his counterparts on the world stage. Some of these relations were marked with abiding personal warmth; others involved an element of wariness; but no leader, in my view, was politically and personally closer to the president than Canada's Brian Mulroney.

Through their four years working side-by-side to manage the historic changes that transpired on their watch, George relied on the prime minister—for advice, for his candid views on the toughest bilateral issues, for acting as a reliable back-channel to other leaders, and most of all for his friendship.

It was a positive, and productive, partnership. The prime minister was a helpful sounding board on dense matters of substance—Open Skies, German Unification, the first Gulf War, the Baltics—as well as matters of style.

For example, it was Brian Mulroney who, early on, encouraged the president to pick up the phone and regularly reach out to his fellow world leaders—even those from the smallest and weakest countries, even if he didn't need something from them. George Bush was already renowned as a virtuoso at the art of personal diplomacy, but Brian's piece of advice added a new dimension.

"What do we talk about?" George asked when Brian first made the suggestion.

"It doesn't matter—talk about the weather if it comes to that," Brian answered, arguing it would help America foster and nurture a spirit of goodwill around the world. Later on, if the West or the United States needed something, those leaders would remember the courtesy and friendship personally extended to them by the president of the United States.

It was also the French-speaking Mulroney who, at key junctures, helped the Bush administration keep the wily and pragmatic François Mitterrand, *Le President de la Republique*, somewhat in line—or at least "on the reservation."

And it was Brian Mulroney who taught President Bush a particularly fascinating reality of international diplomacy, as the prime minister himself has recounted over the first NATO Summit George attended in June of 1989.

The occasion marked the 40th anniversary of the alliance; and with his fellow leaders gathered in Brussels for the formal session, the president unveiled a proposal to reduce conventional forces in Europe. He spoke seriously, but briefly; and understanding the potential for a series of speeches stretching over several hours to veer into extreme tedium, most of the other leaders also kept their remarks as mercifully succinct as they could. Meanwhile, as they spoke, President Bush was eagerly paying attention and even taking notes.

When it came time for the prime minister of Iceland to speak, however, he spoke on, and on, and on—and as he did, George Bush, ever-mindful of his manners, continued to take notes.

Finally, the speeches ended and the meeting was adjourned for a brief break, at which point George sauntered over to Brian and appearing somewhat exasperated asked: "What the hell was that?" He was referring to the fact that, while Iceland is a member of NATO, at the time it had no troops in NATO.

"George," Prime Minister Mulroney said with a wry smile, "you've just learned a key lesson in international summitry: the smaller the country, the longer the speech."

Their friendship was as genuine as it was deep, and the pages that follow chronicle their productive partnership rooted in common values and common aspirations. Of course, it was a singular honour for me to work with these two exceptional men to conceive and advance the North

American Free Trade Agreement—and to advance the cause of free, and fair, trade throughout the world.

It remains my firm belief that open and balanced trade relations with vital allies is essential to the peace and prosperity of both the American and Canadian peoples, and it is my fervent hope that we will continue to learn from the shared vision and leadership this pair of true statesmen established for us.

Chapter 1:

"Tell him, Brian, I will not posture on the Wall"

1989

Introduction

The groundwork for the Bush-Mulroney partnership was laid during the first mandate of the Mulroney Government between 1984 and 1988, when Bush served as Ronald Reagan's vice-president. During this time, the two leaders would consult often, but away from the prying eyes of the news media and over-protective officials.

As the prime minister later disclosed to Doro Bush Koch in an interview for her book, *My Father, My President*: "When I became leader of the Conservative Party in Canada in 1983, I went down to see President Reagan before the '84 Election—and I privately went out to the Naval Observatory (the vice-president's official residence) to see your father. It was a tradition I maintained throughout the second Reagan term. From the very beginning of our relationship, I found him to be a very interested and interesting personality."

"I found him easy to talk to, gregarious and possessed of a great sense of humor ..." Bush observed of the Canadian leader as their friendship developed. "Brian demonstrated that it was possible to be both a strong leader for Canada and a true friend of the United States. When we had disputes on trade or environmental issues, he never backed away from placing Canada's interests first. But even when we had differences over policy, our personal relationship helped us talk about them frankly, and allowed us to try to solve them privately, without public posturing."[1]

Their friendship deepened throughout the second Reagan term to the point that Mulroney was among the very first foreign leaders to track President-elect Bush down at the Houstonian Hotel the night of his White House victory on 8 November 1988. "I was in the middle of my own election campaign, which was held on the 21st of November that year. We had a long

---

1   Bush, George H.W. and Brent Scowcroft. (1998). *A World Transformed: The Collapse of the Soviet Empire, The Unification of Germany, Tiananmen Square, The Gulf War.* New York: Alfred A. Knopf. pp 62–63

and detailed talk that night about what we'd do together if I won my second term—which, happily, I did."

Accordingly, shortly after his inauguration on 20 January 1989, the 41st president made Ottawa the site of his first foreign visit—flying to Canada on 11 February for what he called a "typical brainstorming session" with Mulroney and his team. During that round of consultations, the prime minister made a particularly noteworthy suggestion regarding policy towards the Soviet Union. "Brian asked whether, as part of an effort to counter Gorbachev's public relations offensive, a presidential trip to Eastern Europe might help," Bush recalled. "If I went armed with a comprehensive plan for dealing with the area, and a sense of how to use the symbolism involved, it could be quite a public relations coup of our own—and not necessarily bad for Gorbachev. I thought the trip was a great idea."[2]

In the privacy of his personal journal, Mulroney was himself putting similar thoughts to paper after the Bush visit to Ottawa. "President Bush made a very favourable impression on his first trip here," Mulroney noted. "He was well informed, considerate and thorough—but he displayed a glimmer of steel that I believe characterizes a firm and independent man. For someone who, until recently, had a fuzzy and "wimpish" portrayal— perceptions are invariably inaccurate and unfair—my guess is that George will prove to be perhaps more resolute than his predecessors. He was certainly more aware of all aspects of his brief and spoke knowledgeably for some hours on a variety of intricate matters ranging from NATO negotiations to Japanese trade, without reference to a single note."[3]

Mulroney also left history, again through his personal journal, a description of a 1989 meeting at Kennebunkport between the two men. Their discussions would continue in this matter for the next four years.

"The substantive discussions with President Bush took place over break-fast—bacon, eggs, and coffee—on the outdoor terrace beginning about 7:30 a.m. They broke up some four hours later, interrupted only by appearances by National Security Advisor Brent Scowcroft and Chief of Staff John Sununu. We covered the waterfront: bilateral matters—acid rain, trade irritants, FTA application problems, etc.—and international affairs, where the president was eager to review events in Colombia; how Canada would cooperate in certain aspects of the national strategy to be announced a few days later; our recent rebuff of Panamanian President Noriega; Canada's intention to seek membership in the Organization of American States (which I had not mentioned publicly in Canada); and a follow-up of his major issues flowing from the Paris Summit."[4]

2   Bush and Scowcroft. see *A World Transformed*, p 63.

3   Mulroney, Brian. (2007). *Memoirs*. Toronto: McClelland and Stewart. pp 651–652.

4   Mulroney. see *Memoirs*. p 673–674.

As readers will see, the most crucial matters on the bilateral agenda for the two leaders were the battle against acid rain and the implementation of the Canada–US FTA. In his first speech to Congress, delivered the night before his arrival in Ottawa, Bush had already signaled the willingness of his new administration to go farther than the previous president and administration in moving towards an effective treaty on acid rain between Canada and the US.

On the global agenda, the new US administration was still preparing their approach to the Soviet Union, which formed the basis for most of the talks between Bush and Mulroney in 1989 in the field of international affairs.[5] During a late spring conversation between the two men, in fact, Mulroney suggested that the United States revisit the "Open Skies" proposal first introduced some 30 years before during the Eisenhower administration. Some administration advisors fought the concept, which would offer both countries aerial inspection rights at each other's military installations, as "old hat," but Bush overruled them and embraced the idea. "I didn't feel that Open Skies was such a bad idea—it looked like a no-lose proposition from our side," he later confided. "Gorbachev, committed to *glasnost*, would find it hard from a public-relations standpoint to reject it... I thought we had a lot to gain."[6]

While no one could have predicted it at the time, the Berlin Wall would itself be history by the time 1989 was over. In the aftermath of this dramatic and earth-shattering event, the president sent a private message to Gorbachev through Mulroney when the latter visited the Kremlin for talks with Gorbachev in late November. "Tell him, Brian, I will not posture on the Wall," Bush said.[7]

Mulroney himself has written that Bush's actions—the president's refusal to rhetorically strut triumphantly on the ruins of the Berlin Wall while facing Moscow—was arguably the 41st president's finest moment.[8] More objective voices from the academic arena agree with the former prime minister's assessment. "While his (Bush's) choice to speak only ceremonially on the German question raised objections from some," Professor William Forrest Harlow of Texas Tech University concludes, "Bush's lack of policy-making speech ultimately helped to make sure that Germany was not pulled from the path of democracy. This deliberate silence helped coordinate the efforts of US allies and foes alike, and ultimately proved the correct choice

5   "He (Gorbachev) found "entirely normal" that GB, having been VP for eight years, would want to take an appropriate amount of time to come up with his own policies and approaches for his own administration," Mulroney, writing by hand in his personal journal on a visit to the USSR, noted after talks with Mikhail Gorbachev. See Mulroney. *Memoirs*. pp 701–702.

6   Bush and Scowcroft. see *A World Transformed*. pp 54.

7   Mulroney. see *Memoirs*, pp 699.

8   Mulroney. see *Memoirs*. pp 699.

in Bush's rhetorical management of the fall of the Berlin Wall and eventual German reunification. The Cold War ended without its final battle having to be fought."[9]

Upon his return from Moscow, Mulroney and Bush dined together November 29th as part of the president's consultations for his historic Malta summit with Gorbachev just a few days following. With the dramatic events in Berlin still playing out, the question of what would become of Germany was very much front and centre on everyone's mind. "(Brian) told me that Gorbachev was concerned that (German Chancellor Helmut) Kohl was trying to make 'end runs' around the allies," Bush later observed. "His sense of Gorbachev's view was that 'the Germans could forget about unification' … 'People have died eating unripened fruit,' (Gorbachev) warned."[10]

James McGrath and Arthur Milnes

Remarks and a Question-and-Answer Session With Reporters, Ottawa, Canada 24 Sussex Drive 10 February 1989

The President. Let me just say on behalf of Mrs. Bush, our Secretary of State, and others, this has been a good visit. It is an important visit because it symbolizes the importance that we place on the relationship with Canada. We're each other's largest trading partners. We are friends. We share a long, peaceful border, and we have many common interests. And today we had an opportunity to discuss not just the bilateral relationship that is very, very strong and very good but we had a chance to talk about the East-West relationship. I had a chance to talk about the problems on trade; indeed, our trade ministers are talking right now, you might say. And so, I felt the visit was outstanding.

The prime minister and I reviewed the concerns that he has about acid rain; and I referred him to what I said last night to the American people: my determination to move on forward with setting limits, with legislation, and then moving to discussions with Canada, leading to an accord that I think

9   Harlow, William Forrest. (2006). Chapter 3 "And the Wall Came Tumbling Down: Bush's Rhetoric of Silence during German Reunification." in *The Rhetorical Presidency of George H.W. Bush*. Martin J. Medhurst, ed. College Station: Texas A&M Press. pp 53.

10   Bush and Scowcroft. see *A World Transformed*. p 196

will be beneficial to both countries. And so, that problem—and it has been a problem—is one that we are both determined to move forward towards solution. In terms of the trade agreement, we, of course, have saluted the courageous position taken by the prime minister of Canada. We have great respect for that in the United States; and we want to now do our part, to follow through with whatever implementation is required.

So, the mood was upbeat, the spirit good, and I am very glad that this was my first visit outside of the continental United States as president. And we will keep in touch, and each of us has pledged to see that this strong relationship becomes even stronger.

I think we both agreed we'd take a question or two at what we affectionately call a scrum. [Laughter] I've been looking for words to describe what we do at press occasions like this down across the border, and that's an appropriate word.

Acid Rain

Q. Mr. President, to what degree did you assure the prime minister of your feeling of confidence that the Congress will go along with you on your acid rain request last night?

The President. I think the prime minister is aware of the political divisions and political waves there in our country on this issue. But I assured him that the time for just pure study was over and that we've now approached the time for legislative action. And I pledged that in the campaign. And so, to the degree there is disparity, a lack of uniformity in the Congress, I think the prime minister sees it as my responsibility to try to move forward to do that which I said I wanted to do.

Agricultural and Environmental Issues

Q.—concern that the Arctic blast that just swept across the continent following on last summer's drought has created some permanent damage in the agricultural regions on both sides of the border? I wonder if you discussed that at all and whether there could be a cooperative way of dealing with this and maybe at some point making a proposal to get some of the surplus Canadian water down into the drought-stricken regions of the US?

The President. We did not discuss water diversion. We did not discuss the effects of the Arctic cold air. We did talk about the need for a global approach to environmental concerns.

Acid Rain

Q. Do you have an estimate of how long it will take, assuming the Congress goes along with your legislative programme, before you are ready to talk about a bilateral accord?

The President. No, but we're going to press forward with this right away. We have a brand new administrator of EPA. We've got a legislative team to propose the legislation I talked about last night. And we've gotten some reasonable levels of funding. So, we're on the move. But we did not discuss an exact time frame. I would be misrepresenting or understating things if I didn't say that the prime minister once again impressed on me the urgency of moving as fast as we can, but we didn't set a time.

Q. Yes, sir, you were saying, Mr. President, that you weren't in a position yet to discuss a specific timetable and targets for reduction of acid rain.

The President. We will be discussing targets, and we will get agreement on that, I'm sure. But I have an obligation now to recommend to our Congress the setting of certain limits, so we will move forward with that much specific.

Q. Mr. President, what kind of reductions and what kind of timetable do you have in mind?

The President. I have in mind as fast as possible.

Q. Mr. Prime Minister, I wondered, sir, if you are satisfied with the steps that the president has outlined to deal with the acid rain question or whether you have asked for more here?

The Prime Minister. Well, I think that this represents quite substantial progress. You know, it wasn't so long ago that Canada was sort of going it alone in many ways in this area. The president's position puts a great impetus for action domestically in the United States, which is a condition precedent, and the president is signalling, as well, subsequent discussions that will lead to an acid rain accord to benefit both the United States and Canada. This, I think, is real progress. And while I suppose I'm like a lot of people who would like it done tomorrow in this area, I know it's not going to happen, but this represents a very measurable progress. And I view it as evidence of the commitments that the president gave during the campaign and has referred to since, including his speech to the Congress last night, which is, for a neighbour and friend troubled by this problem for some time, very encouraging.

Q. Presuming you and the president reach an agreement, could you begin to discuss an accord before the full US programme is in place on acid rain, or will it be necessary to wait until its legislation is through Congress?

The Prime Minister. The Americans will, of course, deal with their own problems domestically, free from any comment by me about what happens internally. But clearly, what the president is saying is that he has a two-pronged approach: one that will summon the legislative authority of the Congress of the United States to put in place those mechanisms that are required there; and secondly, an arrangement which will be negotiated with Canada to conclude an accord which will deal, hopefully, in a definitive manner with this.

Q. How soon can those negotiations—

Q. Would you prefer to undertake negotiations immediately with the United States instead of waiting for them first to pass laws?

The Prime Minister. First, it is necessary for the president to talk about this with legislators and that the Americans are prepared to pass their own laws for the purification of their atmosphere in this domain. In the second place, as the president has just indicated, we are on the way to advance, rapidly I hope, towards the conclusion of the negotiations for a bilateral accord about the international environment. Therefore, we are encouraged by the developments and the declarations of President Bush today.

Canadian Steel Exports

Q. Prime Minister, did you discuss the steel issue, and did you make any mention of keeping Canada out of the voluntary export programme that the steel lobby in the United States wants?

The Prime Minister. There is a meeting going on now between Ms. [Carla] Hills [US Trade Representative] and Minister [of International Trade] John Crosbie in regard specifically to that. But as you know, Canada is a fair trader, and we should not in any way be impacted by that kind of proposition. We wouldn't deserve in any way to be included within its purview. And that would be the position that Mr. Crosbie will be explaining to Ms. Hills.

Une dernière question, a final question, Mr. President, and then—

The President. Dernière?

The Prime Minister. Une dernière question pour le president?

The President. Mais oui. [Laughter] *C'est fine pour moi.* [Sure, this is fine for me.] It's colder than hell. Yes, sorry about that. [Laughter]

Acid Rain

Q. In 1995 or the year 2000—for a 50-percent cut in acid rain?

The President. *Qu'est ce que c'est la question?* [What is the question?] *Je ne comprends pas.* [I don't understand.] [Laughter]

Q. Would you like 1995 or the year 2000 for a 50 per cent cut in transporter emissions on acid rain?

The President. Too early to answer that.

Q. Will negotiations start this year, Mr. President?

The President. I hope so.

East-West Relations

Q. Were you on the same wavelength on East-West relations in your discussions this morning?

The President. Certainement! [Laughter]

The Prime Minister. May I introduce my Quebec lieutenant [laughter].

The President. No, we were. And I have great respect for the prime minister's views. I have great respect for his understanding with his experience of the alliance and its importance. I value his judgement on what's happening inside the Soviet Union. And so, we had a long, I think productive, discussion about that. And I had an opportunity to explain to him that our review of our national security policies, our foreign policy objectives—it's a serious thing. It is not a foot-dragging operation. It is not trying to send a signal to Secretary Gorbachev that we want to move backwards. It is simply prudent. And I am absolutely convinced that the Soviets understand this; and I'm also convinced that the—I don't want to put words in his mouth—but the prime minister of Canada, a very important part of all of this, understands it as well.

Remarks and a Question and Answer Session
With Reporters at The White House
4 May 1989

The President. May I just, at the outset of this scrum, in which we each answer questions, say what a joy it's been to have Prime Minister Mulroney back here with his very special Mila. Barbara and I froze them to death on the balcony. It's warm now, but 20 minutes ago, it was cold—temperature; warm in terms of the feeling that existed at that little lunch and, indeed, over in the Oval Office.

And I cite that because the relationship between the United States and Canada remains strong. Our respect for the prime minister and his objectives remains strong. The fact that he fought hard for this breakthrough free trade agreement has the respect for him at an altogether high level. And so, I can report that the conversations that we had that touched on a wide array of subjects—on the environment, and on the importance of the NATO meeting, and on the bilateral relations—was good. And we found that we can look each other in the eye and talk out any differences with no rancour. And we salute him and welcome him as a good friend.

And now, Mr. Prime Minister, the stand-up mike is all yours.

The Prime Minister. Thank you, Mr. President. We had a very delightful and effective meeting, I thought, with President Bush and his colleagues. And Mila and I had an especially delightful lunch with Barbara and the president.

Our discussions today on the agenda dealt with the environment, which is very important, and I applaud the leadership the president is giving to the environment, particularly on the question of acid rain.

We discussed, as well, something that Margaret Thatcher has described as a model for the rest of the world, and that's the Canada–United States Free Trade Agreement, which is in its infancy, is growing and growing strongly, and I think to the benefit of both of our nations.

And we discussed the role of NATO and the importance of the Western alliance in the world—the role of the United States in that alliance. The position of Canada is unequivocal in that regard.

Thank you, sir.

Arms Control

Q. Mr. President, are you willing to compromise your position now on short-range missiles in terms of starting negotiations with the Soviet Union on that area?

The President. I want the NATO summit to be a success. And we will be working with the Germans and with others to see that there is a common NATO position. This is no time for one to compromise or somebody not to compromise. We've made proposals to the Germans; I expect we'll be hearing from them soon. And I'd prefer to do whatever negotiation amongst allies that is required in private, recognizing that we all want the NATO summit to be successful. And there's a lot of public discussion of this issue, and that's fine. I don't plan in detail to join in on that public discussion. The US position is well-known. NATO's last stated public position is well-known. And we're prepared to go from there.

Q. It sounds like you're ready to negotiate.

The President. Well, I'm always willing to negotiate. But we're not going to go for any third zero or getting SNF [Strategic Nuclear Forces] out of whack in terms of negotiations. So, let's be clear on that. But certainly, I'll be willing to discuss these issues, as we did in a very constructive way with the prime minister.

Q. Prime Minister Mulroney, what did you say to the president about the SNF issue?

The Prime Minister. What I said to the president was that NATO was founded on, in my judgement, two concepts: first, solidarity; and secondly, the American leadership of the Western alliance. And it's the solidarity that has brought about the success that the West has engendered thus far. And we have to stick together on all of these fundamental questions, and we will.

NATO is a grouping of sovereign independent nations. There is going to be vigorous debate, unlike the Warsaw Pact. In NATO, there are independent nations who get together, and who come together willingly under a common shield to achieve common objectives. And so, while there has to be this kind of debate, in the end, there must be solidarity, total solidarity. And there must be a common view of leadership, which has served the world so well for 40 years. Now, we're going to Brussels to celebrate the achievements of NATO. And that's exactly what we are going to be doing, and that is why we look forward to President Bush's presence there—to celebrate that particular achievement in which the United States has played such a pivotal role.

Q.—how public opinion in Europe to have NATO—

Q. Did you urge the president to begin negotiations on SNF reductions, sir? Did you urge the president to begin negotiations on SNF reductions?

The Prime Minister. I've just said what the position of Canada is in regard to—there's one NATO position. This is not an association where everybody freelances.

Q.—different views on this, though.

The Prime Minister. We have a common NATO position, and while there are divergence of views that emerge from time to time, the object of our getting together is to harmonize those views into one position. And that's what we're going to be able to do.

North Atlantic Treaty Organization

Q. Mr. President, can we go back to NATO a second?

The President. Yes. For me or—

Q. For you, sir. Mr. President, you were very careful, I thought, to say you didn't want the third zero. That still allows for the possibility of reducing the number of short-range nuclear weapons.

The President. Look, my emphasis will be on conventional force reductions. And we will be talking very soon with the Germans on a proposal we made to them. We've listened very carefully in a very—to the constructive suggestions that Prime Minister Mulroney has raised, and that's really all I care to say about it. I want the NATO meeting to be a success. And one way you guarantee success is not to go out and fine tune nuance differences that may exist between various staunch allies. And so, the German position was made public last week. And I will continue to work with the leaders of the NATO countries to see that we have a successful summit.

Q. Mr. President—

Q. Mr. Prime Minister—

Q. Mr. President, did you discuss a bilateral accord—

The President. Here's what we're going to do to be fair. We're going to rotate these questions. The next one is for the prime minister of Canada—if you want equal time. [Laughter]

The Prime Minister. I don't insist on equal time, Mr. President. [Laughter]

The President. You're entitled to it. You've got to have it.

Acid Rain

Q.—any new commitments on acid rain?

The Prime Minister. I'll take it. [Laughter] All right. We'll rotate.

Q. How about bilateral accords?

The Prime Minister. We'll rotate, but I've got to get a chance to answer. Acid rain—we had an excellent discussion on that. The president has made a very strong statement in regard to his intentions in acid rain, which will involve legislation and cooperation with the Congress. We look forward to that and once that is achieved, we look forward to the conclusion of a mutual accord which will allow our countries to bring to an end, hopefully, a problem that has been a major challenge to both of our governments and one that has blighted the environments of the United States and of Canada. So, we're moving along on that. I'm pleased with what the president had to say today. I met with congressional leaders, including Senator Mitchell, earlier this morning. And as the prime minister of Canada, I'm pleased with the manner in which this very important matter is going.

Health Care in Canada

Q.—about the health system in Canada.

The Prime Minister. Pardon me?

Q. I want to ask you, are you worried about this exodus of doctors from Canada to the United States, where they make more money? Are you worried that that will hurt your wonderful health system in Canada?

The Prime Minister. Well, we're always—we don't like to lose any talented Canadians. But we're very proud of the special health care system that we've developed over the years. It's an integral part of our citizenship. We strengthen it every opportunity we can, and we don't see it under any challenge or attack.

Q. Could you explain that to Mr. Bush so we can get that same health system in the United States?

The Prime Minister. Well, Mr. Bush is very, very well acquainted with the Canadian system, as with others, and I can only speak for ours. I know of your interest in this area. And as far as we're concerned, we've developed our own system, which we prize very highly. Others have their own, of which they're proud, no doubt.

Acid Rain

Q.—about acid rain once again, sir?

Q. Senator Mitchell mentioned this morning that Canada should be pushing for a bilateral accord on acid rain consecutively, while the administration introduces its legislation on acid rain. Was there any talk about that and will you be pushing for that?

The Prime Minister. Well, I think the president knows my position full well. We know that there have to be legislative changes here in the United States to kind of equate the initiatives taken in Canada. And once that is done, or while—in the process of that being done, then there has to be an international accord that is an enforceable document, by which we can measure our progress and enforce delinquency in that event. And so, President Bush is known as a strong environmentalist. He's made some very significant statements in regard to not only acid rain but its impact on our bilateral relationship and his resolve to clean it up. So, I'm very encouraged.

Q. President Bush, can we ask you, sir, about acid rain? Did you make any undertakings in your lunch in terms of what's going to be in your clean air legislation that's going to help this acid rain problem?

The President. We didn't go into the specific amounts. As the prime minister said, he knows of my commitment. He knows now that we are in the final stages of formulating our recommendations to the Congress—the Clean Air Act. And indeed, we'll be prepared, after those recommendations go forward, to discuss in more detail the subject that you're asking about. So, we did have a chance to do what you asked about. And look, if there's anything that the prime minister of Canada has been clear with me about—and he's been clear with me on everything—it is this subject. So, I don't think there's any—he forcefully brings it up, and I tell him where we stand.

Arms Control

Q. Prime Minister Mulroney, the president said you made concrete suggestions on the issue of short-range missiles. Can you give us an idea, sir, what some of those suggestions entailed?

The Prime Minister. Well, Mr. Clark [Canadian Secretary of State for External Affairs] has been in touch with Secretary [of State] Baker and others in regard to how this matter might be broached. We don't—we discuss it privately with our allies and that's what we have tried to do. But the position of Canada—the one I've set out is—it deals with the effectiveness of NATO being predicated on our solidarity and the leadership, a very particular role of leadership, by the United States in that equation. And we think that within those parameters, we can resolve differences of degree and emphasis that will come up from sovereign states from time to time. And we think that this is what the president and I and Secretary Baker and Minister Clark have been working on and will continue to work on.

Acid Rain

Q. Mr. President, your good friend Michael Dukakis said the other day to the prime minister that he expected—he thought that it was possible for an acid rain treaty between Canada and the United States to be signed within a year. I don't know what your feelings are on this, but could you give us kind of a time frame? Do you think it's possible that there might be a treaty signed at least before you leave or the next election?

The President. Well, there will be great progress made. Whether the treaty proves to be the vehicle for demonstrating that progress, I don't know, and I can't say.

Environmental Issues

Q. Mr. Prime Minister, was there any discussion of a global warming convention, and if so, what direction did it take?

The Prime Minister. Yes, the president and I had an excellent discussion of the entire environmental formula. I expressed the view as well that there can be little progress in terms of the environment unless there's a very strong leadership role played by the United States. And I've already indicated to you President Bush's very strong commitment to the environment in all of its related and ancillary and principal dimensions, and this is a very, very important one. But you know, you can hold all the conferences you want, but if the principal players are not there, then progress can be fairly modest. So, President Bush indicated to me, as he did in Ottawa, his intention to play a very significant leadership role in all aspects of the environment, and I think we're all very encouraged by that.

Thank you very much.

The President. Last question for the president—the prime minister having handled his last one beautifully.

China–US Relations

Q. Different subject, on China. Your administration has been very outspoken in promoting democratic efforts in places like Poland and Nicaragua and around the world. But you haven't really said anything about China. Do you have some words of encouragement for the students who are defying a government ban in order to protest in favour of freedom and democracy?

The President. I have words of encouragement for freedom and democracy wherever, and I would like to see progress in China, in the Soviet Union, and in other systems that have heretofore not been in the forefront, to put it mildly, of human rights or of democratic rights. And I wouldn't suggest to any leadership of any country that they accept every demand by every group. But I will say that as I reviewed what the demands are today, we can certainly, as the United States, identify with them. When they talk about more free press, we would encourage that, wherever it might be. When they talk about—I forget what the list was of every demand, but a lot of them had my enthusiastic backing, in a broad, generic sense. And I would like to encourage China or the Soviet Union or other totalitarian countries—countries that have not enjoyed democratic practices—to move as quick as they can down democracy's path.

And I've been pleased with some of the changes in China. It's changed dramatically since I was living there. But they've got a ways to go, and other countries in this hemisphere have a long ways to go, and countries over in Europe have a long way to go. And so, I would encourage them all: democracy is on the move. And this is one thing that the prime minister and I talked about. When we go to that NATO meeting, we're going to be on the side that is winning and the side that is right, fundamentally right. Freedom, democracy, human rights, these are the things we stand for. So, I would encourage every government to move as quickly as they can to achieve human rights.

President George H.W. Bush
Remarks at the Texas A&M University
Commencement Ceremony at College Station
12 May 1989

We are reminded that no generation can escape history. Parents, we share a fervent desire for our children and their children to know a better world, a safer world. And students, your parents and grandparents have lived through a world war and helped America to rebuild the world. They witnessed the drama of postwar nations divided by Soviet subversion and force, but sustained by an allied response most vividly seen in the Berlin airlift. And today I would like to use this joyous and solemn occasion to speak to you and to the rest of the country about our relations with the Soviet Union. It is fitting that these remarks be made here at Texas A&M University.

Wise men—Truman and Eisenhower, Vandenberg and Rayburn, Marshall, Acheson, and Kennan—crafted the strategy of containment. They believed that the Soviet Union, denied the easy course of expansion, would turn inward and address the contradictions of its inefficient, repressive, and inhumane system. And they were right—the Soviet Union is now publicly facing this hard reality. Containment worked. Containment worked because our democratic principles and institutions and values are sound and always have been. It worked because our alliances were, and are, strong and because the superiority of free societies and free markets over stagnant socialism is undeniable.

We are approaching the conclusion of an historic postwar struggle between two visions: one of tyranny and conflict and one of democracy and freedom. The review of US–Soviet relations that my administration has just completed outlines a new path toward resolving this struggle. Our goal is bold, more ambitious than any of my predecessors could have thought possible. Our review indicates that 40 years of perseverance have brought us a precious opportunity, and now it is time to move beyond containment to a new policy for the 1990s—one that recognizes the full scope of change taking place around the world and in the Soviet Union itself. In sum, the United States now has as its goal much more than simply containing Soviet expansionism. We seek the integration of the Soviet Union into the community of nations. And as the Soviet Union itself moves toward greater openness and democratization, as they meet the challenge of responsible international behavior, we will match their steps with steps of our own. Ultimately, our objective is to welcome the Soviet Union back into the world order.

The Soviet Union says that it seeks to make peace with the world and criticizes its own postwar policies. These are words that we can only applaud, but a new relationship cannot simply be declared by Moscow or bestowed by others; it must be earned. It must be earned because promises are never enough. The Soviet Union has promised a more cooperative relationship before, only to reverse course and return to militarism. Soviet foreign policy has been almost seasonal: warmth before cold, thaw before freeze. We seek a friendship that knows no season of suspicion, no chill of distrust.

We hope *perestroika* is pointing the Soviet Union to a break with the cycles of the past—a definitive break. Who would have thought that we would see the deliberations of the Central Committee on the front page of *Pravda* or dissident Andrei Sakharov seated near the councils of power? Who would have imagined a Soviet leader who canvasses the sidewalks of Moscow and also Washington, DC? These are hopeful, indeed, remarkable signs. And let no one doubt our sincere desire to see *perestroika*, this reform, continue and succeed. But the national security of America and our allies is not predicated on hope. It must be based on deeds, and we look for enduring, ingrained economic and political change.

While we hope to move beyond containment, we are only at the beginning of our new path. Many dangers and uncertainties are ahead. We must not forget that the Soviet Union has acquired awesome military capabilities. That was a fact of life for my predecessors, and that's always been a fact of life for our allies. And that is a fact of life for me today as President of the United States.

As we seek peace, we must also remain strong. The purpose of our military might is not to pressure a weak Soviet economy or to seek military superiority. It is to deter war. It is to defend ourselves and our allies and to do something more: to convince the Soviet Union that there can be no reward in pursuing expansionism, to convince the Soviet Union that reward lies in the pursuit of peace.

Western policies must encourage the evolution of the Soviet Union toward an open society. This task will test our strength. It will tax our patience, and it will require a sweeping vision. Let me share with you my vision: I see a Western Hemisphere of democratic, prosperous nations, no longer threatened by a Cuba or a Nicaragua armed by Moscow. I see a Soviet Union as it pulls away from ties to terrorist nations like Libya that threaten the legitimate security of their neighbors. I see a Soviet Union which respects China's integrity and returns the northern territories to Japan, a prelude to the day when all the great nations of Asia will live in harmony.

But the fulfilment of this vision requires the Soviet Union to take positive steps, including: First, reduce Soviet forces. Although some small steps have already been taken, the Warsaw Pact still possesses more than

30,000 tanks, more than twice as much artillery, and hundreds of thousands more troops in Europe than NATO. They should cut their forces to less threatening levels, in proportion to their legitimate security needs.

Second, adhere to the Soviet obligation, promised in the final days of World War II, to support self-determination for all the nations of Eastern Europe and central Europe. And this requires specific abandonment of the Brezhnev doctrine. One day it should be possible to drive from Moscow to Munich without seeing a single guard tower or a strand of barbed wire. In short, tear down the Iron Curtain.

And third, work with the West in positive, practical—not merely rhetorical—steps toward diplomatic solution to these regional disputes around the world. I welcome the Soviet withdrawal from Afghanistan, and the Angola agreement. But there is much more to be done around the world. We're ready. Let's roll up our sleeves and get to work.

And fourth, achieve a lasting political pluralism and respect for human rights. Dramatic events have already occurred in Moscow. We are impressed by limited, but freely contested elections. We are impressed by a greater toleration of dissent. We are impressed by a new frankness about the Stalin era. Mr. Gorbachev, don't stop now!

And fifth, join with us in addressing pressing global problems, including the international drug menace and dangers to the environment. We can build a better world for our children.

As the Soviet Union moves toward arms reduction and reform, it will find willing partners in the West. We seek verifiable, stabilizing arms control and arms reduction agreements with the Soviet Union and its allies. However, arms control is not an end in itself but a means of contributing to the security of America and the peace of the world. I directed Secretary [of State] Baker to propose to the Soviets that we resume negotiations on strategic forces in June and, as you know, the Soviet Union has agreed.

Our basic approach is clear. In the strategic arms reductions talks, we wish to reduce the risk of nuclear war. And in the companion defence and space talks, our objective will be to preserve our options to deploy advanced defences when they're ready. In nuclear testing, we will continue to seek the necessary verification improvements in existing treaties to permit them to be brought into force. And we're going to continue to seek a verifiable global ban on chemical weapons. We support NATO efforts to reduce the Soviet offensive threat in the negotiations on conventional forces in Europe. And as I've said, fundamental to all of these objectives is simple openness.

Make no mistake, a new breeze is blowing across the steppes and the cities of the Soviet Union. Why not, then, let this spirit of openness grow, let more barriers come down. Open emigration, open debate, open airwaves—

let openness come to mean the publication and sale of banned books and newspapers in the Soviet Union. Let the 19,000 Soviet Jews who emigrated last year be followed by any number who wish to emigrate this year. And when people apply for exit visas, let there be no harassment against them. Let openness come to mean nothing less than the free exchange of people and books and ideas between East and West.

And let it come to mean one thing more. Thirty-four years ago, President Eisenhower met in Geneva with Soviet leaders who, after the death of Stalin, promised a new approach toward the West. He proposed a plan called Open Skies, which would allow unarmed aircraft from the United States and the Soviet Union to fly over the territory of the other country. This would open up military activities to regular scrutiny and, as President Eisenhower put it, "convince the world that we are lessening danger and relaxing tension." President Eisenhower's suggestion tested the Soviet readiness to open their society, and the Kremlin failed that test.

Now, let us again explore that proposal, but on a broader, more intrusive and radical basis—one which I hope would include allies on both sides. We suggest that those countries that wish to examine this proposal meet soon to work out the necessary operational details, separately from other arms control negotiations. Such surveillance flights, complementing satellites, would provide regular scrutiny for both sides. Such unprecedented territorial access would show the world the true meaning of the concept of openness. The very Soviet willingness to embrace such a concept would reveal their commitment to change.

Where there is cooperation, there can be a broader economic relationship; but economic relations have been stifled by Soviet internal policies. They've been injured by Moscow's practice of using the cloak of commerce to steal technology from the West. Ending discriminatory treatment of US firms would be a helpful step. Trade and financial transactions should take place on a normal commercial basis.

And should the Soviet Union codify its emigration laws in accord with international standards and implement its new laws faithfully, I am prepared to work with Congress for a temporary waiver of the Jackson-Vanik Amendment, opening the way to extending most favored nation trade status to the Soviet Union… The policy I have just described has everything to do with you. Today you graduate. You're going to start careers and families, and you will become the leaders of America in the next century. And what kind of world will you know? Perhaps the world order of the future will truly be a family of nations.

It's a sad truth that nothing forces us to recognize our common humanity more swiftly than a natural disaster. I'm thinking, of course, of Soviet Armenia just a few months ago, a tragedy without blame, warlike devastation without war. Our son took our 12-year-old grandson to Yerevan. At the end of the day of comforting the injured and consoling the bereaved, the father and son went to church, sat down together in the midst of the ruins, and wept. How can our two countries magnify this simple expression of caring? How can we convey the good will of our people?

Forty-three years ago, a young lieutenant by the name of Albert Kotzebue, the class of 1945 at Texas A&M, was the first American soldier to shake hands with the Soviets at the bank of the Elbe River. Once again, we are ready to extend our hand. Once again, we are ready for a hand in return. And once again, it is a time for peace.

News Conference, the President and the Prime Minister
Kennebunkport, Maine
31 August 1989

The President. Barbara and I have just been delighted to have the prime minister and Mrs. Mulroney here. And we had a chance this morning— it started out as just a chat, and ended up spending close to four hours talking about issues affecting not only US-Canada but a wide array of issues affecting the whole world, as a matter of fact. As usual, I've learned a lot from the prime minister, and we've really had a substantive discussion. John Sununu and Brent Scowcroft dropped in for some of the discussion. And I can say this—and I'll let the prime minister have equal time—that the relationship between the United States and Canada, a most significant and important relationship, is in good shape.

I have found, just in the short time that I've been in this job, and with respect to the—certainly the prime minister with much more experience in leading a country than I—but I have found that I can either pick up the phone and talk to him with a frankness that is very important, or in a visit of this nature, which we deliberately billed as a private visit, talk to him with no holds barred. We agree on almost all the major issues. And where Canada and the US may have bumps in the road, we can talk very frankly. He is always very frank with me, expressing the Canadian point of view so strongly, and gives me a chance to understand that position. And of course, I feel no inhibitions in telling him where the United States is coming from. And though we have a few more hours of this most pleasant visit—from my standpoint at least and, thus, from the standpoint of the United States, it's been an unusually productive visit. And I'm just again, Brian, so pleased, sir, that you are here.

The Prime Minister. Thank you, Mr. President. Thank you, George.

Well, I really am here to give you the impartial international assessment of the fact that there are no fish out there. [Laughter] I can certify to that. It's not the president's fault there are none—at least not for awhile, at least not for awhile. [Laughter]

Well, we've had a very pleasant and productive visit. Mila and I and the children have enjoyed the hospitality, and we of course enjoy the Bushes and their family a great deal. And so, we had a good opportunity, beginning at breakfast this morning, to really—the President and I—to review important bilateral relations between Canada and the United States from the environment to trade. And then, in the course of kind of an unscheduled next couple of hours, to get more and more into international issues, some of which flow from the Paris summit, others which the president has initiated or seeks to initiate.

And Canada views this relationship as a very special one. We have the largest trading relationship in the world between our two countries, and we have currents of history and bonds of friendship that are, I suspect, unrivalled anywhere. And so, this is an indication of the value of the friendship; this is an occasion for us, as well, to seek to improve it.

. We have challenges and tensions from time to time. And the best way to deal with them is in a straightforward way, and that's exactly what we've done. And I thank the president for his hospitality, which we've greatly enjoyed.

Thank you very much, Mr. President.

The President. Merci [Thank you].

Now, any questions? And why don't we do like we did before, if it's agreeable, sir—just alternate.

Situation in Panama and Colombia

Q. Mr. President, can you tell us why you sent the State Department to make a case against Noriega at the OAS? Given the OAS's history of inaction, is that wasting our time, sir?

The President. No. Working to be sure that all the countries in the OAS understand why we feel as we do about Noriega is very important. And I am not going to give up on multilateral diplomacy. I am going to continue to work with the leaders in this hemisphere, most of whom feel as I do about Noriega, to see if we can't help the Panamanian people get what they deserve; and that is a democratic society that stems from free, fair elections.

And so, we are going to continue to press the case in OAS and every other way.

Q. But they didn't come through for you before.

The President. Keep working on it; keep working the problem.

Q. Did the president discuss the president's new drug strategy, and did he specifically ask Canada to perhaps help in terms of furnishing more money and law enforcement officers to attack the drug cartel operators in Colombia?

The Prime Minister. Well, first, I should say that I share the president's view about General Noriega, and the Government of Canada has conveyed that view directly to the general in recent days. And Secretary of State Joe Clark has issued a strong statement about our view of Panama. We're very supportive of what not only President Bush but all freedom-loving people seek in respect of Panama. And the fact that it hasn't happened yet doesn't mean we shouldn't stop.

With regard to the problem in Colombia, Canada views the statements of the president as the statements of a very courageous—very courageous man—deserving of support not only by the United States but by all industrialized countries, and particularly all nations in this hemisphere. And we have communicated ourselves, of course, with the Government of Colombia; we expect that we will be hearing from them shortly.

The president and I discussed a number of initiatives this morning that we'll be discussing with friends and allies to try and have a more definite impact. The United States will, I suppose, respond on a bilateral basis; and so will Canada. But where there is complete agreement between the president and myself is the need to support a very courageous leader in Colombia and the need to stomp out, by every reasonable means, the terror of drugs which is devastating society in the United States and having a very serious impact as well on Canadians and people around the world.

Q.—a multilateral force to be used to help stamp out those drug traffickers in Colombia?

The President. The main thing is to cooperate with President Barco in the ways that he feels are most effective. That's the best thing. There is no point in Canada or the United States or the Group of Seven [economic summit participants] or any individual country or group of countries imposing its will on a country that is now trying very, very hard to rid itself of this menace. And so, I know that I—the prime minister and I have discussed this—we would be guided by requests from President Barco in Colombia.

Canada–US Relations

Q. Mr. President, what areas would you say the bilateral relations have been unusually productive in these talks? And also, in what areas do you think there still remain some bumps in the road, as you referred to earlier?

The President. Well, look, on the whole area of trade, because the prime minister stood firm in a tough political context for a free trade agreement, dramatic progress has been made. There are still bumps in the road. There are going to still be areas that he and I need to discuss and that our trade representatives need to discuss, to iron these bumps out. And so, the broad area of agreement is relating to the free trade agreement itself, and then where we have disagreements there's going to be a case-by-case looking at problems.

We talked, for example, about a specific: There's been a fishing problem between Canada and the United States regarding lobsters. It's a matter of some concern to me. Well, we decided, look, let's talk about it frankly, refer it to our experts, and then get on with solving it. So, he has been in the forefront of change for environmental protection. And we've come forward now in the United States, trying to have a package that I would encourage our Congress to pass that would do something about acid rain, for example. But again, problems still remain until we put into effect our legislation and then move forward even further with Canada.

So, where we have broad agreements, trade agreements, there are bound to be matters as we go down the road, that are going to need to be ironed out. In terms of the Group of Seven, in terms of the East-West relations, in terms of how we look at matters south of the United States border—and I'm talking about Panama, for example—I find that the prime minister and I, and Canada and the United States, are very, very much in accord. And there are other issues where we may have differences, but in these broad ones, there's agreement, and the problems come on some of the specifics. But amongst friends we can hammer out those difficulties.

Colombia

Q. You talked about support for President Barco, but are there specifics in a Canadian programme that would in any way be coordinated with the US, or is there a separate Canadian programme?

The Prime Minister. Canada's already assisting Colombia in a substantial way, in terms of the administration of the—or improving the system of justice internally within Colombia. Our security forces have been providing assistance and technology, as well. The president and I explored other possibilities where, either individually or collectively, we could be of greater assistance in responding to what is clearly a very courageous and brave voice coming from Colombia asking for understanding and support. But as the president pointed out, it is important that the definition of that agenda come from Colombia and not from us. It is up to the president to indicate to the United States, to Canada, and to friendly neighbours around the world, how we best might be of help.

Q. Mr. President, you can make suggestions to President Barco. After all, this is an American crisis, too. Can't you make suggestions, and would that include some sort of multilateral force, possibly not military, possibly some sort of—I don't know—you talked about the Group of Seven—Interpol, or something like that? And also, have you considered the possibility of some sort of South American summit which would include the Peruvian and Bolivian leaders?

The President. There has been discussion of an anti-narcotic summit. Indeed, I talked to President Barco about that the other day. I feel totally free to make suggestions to him. But all I'm saying is that we must be sensitive, as this man goes to work and has rolled up his sleeves and is putting a lot at risk, that we not be counterproductive in our efforts to help him. But I feel free in talking to him to discuss any subject.

And I've made clear to him... in my last conversation with him, that, please, let us know what in addition that we might do to help. But I think you have to be sensitive in understanding the history in this hemisphere, and you cannot try to impose a solution on a country that is struggling very hard on their own—with international help—to solve this problem.

Q. Given their longstanding antipathy to American military intervention, would it be more acceptable to act in a multilateral way—with the Group of Seven, for example?

The President. Well, there's no question that multilateralism makes great sense in trying to help. But if the question implies intervention of a multilateral force, there again, if requested—

Q. I'm not asking that. At the invitation—

The President. Oh, no question, no question that that would be better. And from our standpoint, it would be better, as it affects the neighbours of Colombia. But again, I don't want to—just through even responding to your question—to appear to be pushing a solution on a man who has dug in there, whose ministers are coordinating their efforts now, and to do something or say something that would be counterproductive and turn public opinion that's now mobilized in Colombia against President Barco's efforts. But, yes—I'm sorry I missed the question—but, yes, I think an international effort on whatever line it is—aid, help of any kind—would be useful.

Canada–US Trade

Q. Prime Minister, could you elaborate from your point of view on the lobster issue what Canada might do? And secondly, how you would characterize what bumps in the road you see there are in the bilateral relationship—trade, environment, whatever?

The Prime Minister. Well, the president was big on lobsters today. I was big on pork because we feel that the Americans have just imposed an unfair tariff on pork. And we discussed the manner in which this will be resolved through the mechanisms provided for the Free Trade Agreement. But we went through a number of issues like that.

But I also point out the president's recent actions, for example, with regard to steel imports into the United States as they affect Canada, which indicates the strong commitment towards liberalized trade, towards removing inhibitions, and towards the belief that freer trade means greater economic growth for both sides... Between our two countries—we do the largest trade in history between two countries, and at the end of the year it's roughly in balance, as opposed to huge imbalances that surge in America's trade relations with other partners.

So, we covered the entire—well, I shouldn't say the entire spectrum, but we covered a good bit of it. And as I say, the president was strong on lobsters and not so good on pork—[laughter]—but we'll change that.

Acid Rain

Q. Mr. Mulroney, on acid rain—

The Prime Minister. I'm sorry, may I just—acid rain—very much so. We covered it, and we're getting to a solution because of the president's initiatives, for which we're very grateful. But we want a bilateral clean air accord between Canada and the United States. And the president and I discussed that as well. And that will move ahead concurrent with the action in this regard in the American Congress. I won't be satisfied that the issue is resolved until President Bush and I sit down and sign that accord. And then that will be an important day.

Q. Do you think you're any closer to an accord now?

The Prime Minister. Yes.

Visit of Prime Minister Mulroney

Q. Prime Minister, can you describe what you've done in terms of recreational activities? Did the president challenge you to a game of tennis?

The Prime Minister. To his great regret. [Laughter]

The President. Now, wait just a minute for clarification. [Laughter]

The Prime Minister. The wind, however, intervened, preventing me from inflicting great damage on his reputation. [Laughter] So, we haven't gotten around to that. But we've been swimming—we've been out in the boat—

The President. Horseshoes this afternoon.

The Prime Minister. —a little fishing—by me, unsuccessfully. [Laughter] So, we've had a good time, full time.

Drug Flow Across the Canadian Border

Q. What about the flow of drugs across the US–Canadian border? How serious a problem is that?

The President. Is this for the prime minister or for me?

Q. Yes, for the prime minister and for you, Mr. President. The flow of drugs across the US–Canadian border—how serious a problem do you regard that as being? And are you prepared to ask for American aid in bolstering your forces along that border? And, Mr. Bush, are you prepared to supply that aid? Was that discussed?

The Prime Minister. Well, there are lots of problems, and I suppose that's one of them, but it's not really a major, major one when you rank it alongside the others. The fact of the matter is that we have a growing problem of our own in Canada, which is one of abuse of this substance, the same way as the United States has. Canada is becoming a progressively important dropping-off area of drugs destined for the United States. And we have been working very actively to interdict those drugs destined not only for Canadians but for trans-shipment into the United States, and with some considerable success.

There's a great deal of cooperation, a very intimate degree of association and cooperation, between all agencies in the United States and in Canada. And the interdiction is very, very successful at the Canadian–American borders. And would the same situation prevail elsewhere, we'd be in better shape.

But as the president pointed out, if you have a country the size of ours or a smaller one, as long as you have access by ports, by air to that, you can trans-ship drugs directed for the United States. And it's our obligation to be as severe and as rigorous as we can in interdicting shipments destined for the United States as—with the same enthusiasm or the same vigour as we apply to trying to stop shipments to our own people.

Colombia

Q. Mr. Prime Minister, would you consider an aid package to Colombia if it was requested similar to what the United States is contemplating, to what President Bush is planning?

The Prime Minister. The drug problem in Canada takes its origin in producing nations. And the producer who is in the process of destroying the young Canadian is exactly the same who's destroying the young American—exactly. He is the same venal, corrupt individual who seeks to profit by destroying young people in all our societies. And so, Canada will—Canada already is being helpful to Colombia. But if the president of Colombia were to ask us for further assistance, either as members of the G-7 or simply in a bilateral relationship, we would respond. And we would respond with enthusiasm because we don't see this as an American problem or a Colombian problem; this is a problem of any decent human being who wants to keep this cancer out of his or her society.

Visit of Prime Minister Mulroney

Q. What is the highlight of the visit for you?

The President. The highlight? Well, I don't know that I can single one thing out, but if it does nothing else, it symbolizes the friendly relationship that we have with Canada. And I am determined that as long as I am president, I will never take for granted friends. It is very important, from what I need to learn to do my job better, to stay in touch with Prime Minister Mulroney. And this visit has been as good, if not better, than the other such visits we've had, even when I was vice president. We had a relationship where we could talk very, very frankly. We could get out our disagreements, as well as the things we agreed on—no acrimony. And he's had a lot of experience in these G-7 meetings and in other international meetings; and I find it extraordinarily helpful to me to just bounce ideas off him—and maybe vice versa—when it comes to East-West relations; when it comes to the changes in Eastern Europe; when it comes to what's happening in Central America, or indeed, in Asia.

And so, the highlight is not only the personal chemistry that I think is good but the fact that we can talk as neighbours in a very unfettered way about a wide array of problems without fearing that we're going to have some misunderstanding or some leak, or something that's going to embarrass either one of us. And that is important. That is a very important point.

Canadian Lobster Exports

Q. Mr. Mulroney, what do you say to the American lobstermen who say you're killing their prices by having your people catch these puny lobsters and then export them here before they're able to grow big enough to reproduce? What do you say to us?

The Prime Minister. Well, the president made a very strong case in respect to that this morning, and he advanced some persuasive arguments that I have instructed my officials to begin examining. And this matter, which is very important to the United States, will be resolved in much the same manner as we seek to resolve others: in a friendly, constructive spirit. We didn't resolve it today, but the president certainly made a very, as I say, persuasive case, as I hope I did in other areas.

President's Vacation

Q. No more fishing?

The President. Oh, yes. Would you like a fishing assessment? Would you really like to know—

Q. Yes. [Laughter]

The President. I told you what I thought yesterday, and this is getting out of hand. And so, between now and when I leave on Monday, I guarantee you— I positively guarantee you that this jinx will be broken. I've seen a lot of good .350 hitters bat about .178 for a while. Then they come out of the slump and move forward. My record fishing in these waters is well-known. It's a superb record, a record of bountiful catches. And somehow, something's gone wrong for the last 13 days—[laughter]—something's happened. But I promise you—I promise you that—in fact, we're thinking of having a poll to take a media person with us when Barbara and I go out to thwart these evil rumours that I don't know what I'm doing fishing. It's gotten out of hand. When I see it on national television, I know we've got to put an end to this monkey business. So, we will prevail. And besides that, everyone knows fishing is a team sport. [Laughter]

The Prime Minister. I just want to issue a formal denial here. It is not the case that there are out in the bay Canadian frogmen with Nova Scotia salmon ready to put on anybody's line. [Laughter]

The President. I hope they will be.

Statement by Press Secretary Marlin Fitzwater on the President's Telephone Conversations With Allied Leaders 17 November 1989

President Bush this morning telephoned the President of France, François Mitterrand, to discuss his views on the upcoming Malta meeting and events in Eastern Europe. President Bush wanted the unique perspective provided by the French president. They discussed a number of issues regarding the impact of recent events in Eastern Europe on the countries of Western Europe. The two presidents agreed to talk again after the EC [European Communities] summit and before the Malta meeting.

President Bush also called the Prime Minister of Canada, Brian Mulroney, to discuss the Malta meeting and his views on these issues. President Bush and Prime Minister Mulroney have very similar thinking on these issues. President Bush and Prime Minister Mulroney will talk again after the Malta meeting.

In addition, Chancellor Kohl of West Germany telephoned President Bush this morning to discuss the events in his country and Eastern Europe.

Remarks Following Discussions Between the President and the Prime Minister
The White House
29 November 1989

The President. Let me just say that Prime Minister Mulroney has very generously come down here and given us a very full briefing—his observations from a long and detailed trip that he took to the Soviet Union. I don't know why he is not more wiped out by jet lag, because I last saw him just a few weeks ago in Central America—he'd come from Asia. Now he's been to the Soviet Union—but it was most generous, Mr. Prime Minister, for you to come here. And on behalf of the Secretary of State and Brent Scowcroft, John Sununu, those of us who will be in the meetings, I can't tell you how much I appreciate your advice and your observations.

Vice President George Bush famously received an earful about acid rain from Prime Minister Brian Mulroney in Ottawa, January 1987.

*In April 1988 Brian Mulroney became only the second Canadian
Prime Minister to address a joint session of the US Congress.
He was introduced by Vice President George Bush.*

The new President's first foreign trip was to Ottawa in February 1989.

G-7 leaders at the Louvre, July 1989.

The two leaders throwing out ceremonial first pitches at the SkyDome, Toronto.

Behind the scenes at the Houston G-7 Summit hosted by President Bush July 1990.

Bush and Mulroney with Margaret Thatcher of the United Kingdom, Helmut Kohl of Germany, François Mitterrand of France, Jacques Delors of the European Community, Giulio Andreotti of Italy and Toshiki Kaifu of Japan.

With Iraqi forces having just invaded Kuwait, the PM and the President held consultations early in the crisis in the White House Residence. They are joined here by senior assistants Stanley Hartt and Lawrence Eagleburger.

Fishing in the waters off Kennebunkport, Maine, 1990.

The fall of the Berlin Wall and the design of the new Europe brought the two North American leaders across the Atlantic many times. Here they are joined by Secretary of State James Baker III, White House Chief of Staff John Sununu and National Security Advisor Gen. Brent Scowcroft.

Chapter 2:

A Remarkable Display of Solidarity

1990

Introduction

George H.W. Bush and Brian Mulroney surely drove respective members of their bureaucracies to distraction. While many at "Foggy Bottom" in Washington and at Ottawa's Pearson Building were trained in the traditional practice of diplomacy that featured the slow and true—immaculately prepared briefing notes, position papers and endless correspondence—the principals in the Canadian-American relationship from 1989 to early 1993 were firm practitioners of leader-to-leader personal diplomacy. If the briefing notes and papers were lacking, both the president and his colleague in Ottawa would simply pick up the telephone and call throughout the world in their quest for information.

General Brent Scowcroft, Bush's trusted national security advisor, summed it up this way: "President Bush invested an enormous amount of time in personal diplomacy, and, in my opinion, it was indispensable to the success of our foreign policy... The president called his principal allies and friends often, frequently not with any particular issue in mind but just to chat and exchange views on how things were going in general... Almost every day there would be such calls..."[11]

Defense Secretary Robert Gates, then Bush's deputy national security advisor, added: "This had never been done before, and in fact some of the foreign leaders thought they were phony calls at first... It took probably a year and a half before we had some of the procedures smoothed out..."[12]

For his part, Mulroney's chief of staff, Hugh Segal, later provided a fascinating glimpse of his prime minister at work internationally with only a telephone in hand (aided of course by the operators in the Prime Minister's Office's communications unit). His account describes Canada's prime

---

11   See Bush and, Scowcroft. *A World Transformed.* p 61.

12   Bush Koch, Doro. (2006). *My Father, My President: A Personal Account of the Life of George H.W. Bush.* New York, Boston: Warner Books. p 283.

minister deftly practicing the art of personal diplomacy at a time of world crisis during the period of the attempted coup against Mikhail Gorbachev in 1991. Segal was on hand in 1991 as the senior members of Canada's foreign, defence and intelligence services gathered to brief Mulroney on the events in the Soviet Union.

"As the group droned on," Segal wrote, "I realized that what they were offering was little more than a distillation of [news sources] which the prime minister himself would have read by six o'clock that morning. Then Mulroney proceeded to brief them! Mulroney had been on the phone overnight to Eastern Europe, London, and Paris and to George Bush in Washington. He had gotten through to people he had met on visits to Russia and had put together a compilation of who was who and what was what, all with far greater detail than the information offered by those around the table."[13]

Both men would put their diplomatic skills to the test, with great success, when Saddam Hussein's tanks and army rolled into Kuwait during the summer of 1990. At an emergency meeting at the White House at the dawn of the crisis in the Middle East, to joint phone calls made by both men to fellow leaders around the world while Bush and Mulroney were at Kennebunkport together at the end of August 1990, and in person-to-person efforts at multilateral gatherings like the United Nations' Conference on Children in New York City that fall, they worked tirelessly together to assemble the coalition that removed Hussein from Kuwait.

Importantly, this partnership between an American president and a Canadian prime minister, in a matter of intense importance to the United Nations and the world, produced results beyond the liberation of Kuwait and the containment of Hussein. In the aftermath of Operation Desert Storm, some saw fit to criticize Bush's decision not to "go to Baghdad" and depose the Iraqi government; but it is precisely because the US and its coalition partners abided by the United Nations Security Council resolutions that they reaped a windfall of political capital. In turn, Bush used this enhanced credibility and international standing to launch the Madrid Peace Conference in October 1991 that laid the foundation for the Oslo Accords two years hence.

James McGrath and Arthur Milnes

---

13   Segal, Hugh. (1996). *No Surrender: Reflections of a Happy Warrior in the Tory Cause*. Toronto: Harper&Collins. pp 145–146.

Reflections, George H.W. Bush
German Re-unification
February 1990
A World Transformed

Brian Mulroney supported reunification but had some reservations. "I'm concerned personally that unification for Germany appears to be fuelled not just by the legitimate desire of the two states to come together," he said, but 'by the total collapse of the economy of one state and the economic strength of another. ... I told (West German Foreign Minister) Genscher, "you're not really talking about a merger here; this is a takeover." He predicted that the real problems with unification would appear further down the road, in areas like the Common Market. "The Community was never designed with the possibility of having such a great European power in mind," he said. I saw these concerns as additional headaches to sort out, but I was not really worried about them.

I told Brian about the suggestion that we allow Soviet troops to stay in East Germany. "It gives me heartburn, though, if we suddenly, in an effort to get German stability, acquiesce in or advocate Soviet troops remaining in Germany," I said. 'That is what we have been against all these years.' Mulroney reacted strongly. "I don't see how, in fairness, we can accept that. The minimum price for German unity should be full German membership in NATO and full support in all the Western organizations and full support for American leadership in the alliance. I indicated to Genscher... and I will tell you: we are not renting our seat in Europe. We paid for it. If people want to know how Canada paid for its seat in Europe, they should check out the graves in Belgium and France... NATO got us this far. Solidarity in the alliance will get us further." Brian was right on target.

Notes For An Address
By The Right Honourable Brian Mulroney
Prime Minister Of Canada
Open Skies Conference
Ottawa
12 February 1990

I am pleased to welcome you to Canada to this conference on Open Skies. We are living remarkable years in world history. The Berlin Wall is down. Nelson Mandela is free. A new age is born.

Throughout Eastern Europe, governments are grappling with the unfamiliar challenges of democracy and economic change. They are trying to accomplish in months what it has taken others decades, even centuries, to achieve. Fulfilling the dreams of a nation for democratic government and satisfying the expectations of a people for new opportunity and prosperity for themselves and their children are historic tasks. They demand time, patience and a great resolve.

In spite of the experience of others, no one can prescribe a road to certain success, nor a route that avoids either great national difficulty or considerable individual sacrifice. New national structures and economies are built slowly. But all nations have a stake in the success of the new governments and an interest in responding constructively to their needs. Canada stands ready to do its part.

Fully 15 per cent of Canadians have their origins in Central and Eastern Europe. These Canadians are schooled in the management of government in a bilingual nation and a multicultural society. And they are experienced in the conduct of international business in a free enterprise world. Canada is committed to cooperate in the re-building of Eastern Europe.

Canada is, also, ready to play its part in building a new international order. For almost half a century there has been half a peace, based in distrust and built on deterrence. Confidence was impossible while basic values were in conflict. But the confrontation of ideologies has, at last, subsided. We are no longer hostage to the frozen political meteorology of suspicion and animosity. The Cold War is over.

Today, in Ottawa, former adversaries work together to ensure that such a long and bitter winter never comes again. The conditions exist now to make a new start on building a better world. The infernal nuclear legacy of the past remains. And unresolved issues and ancient conflicts, forgotten for a while, are exposed now by the sunlight of the *perestroika* thaw.

But, in recent months, much common ground has also reappeared. These developments raise profound questions—about the most effective means of reinforcing political and economic progress in Central and Eastern Europe; about the evolution of the European Community and the unification of Germany; about the risk to stability of dormant conflicts re-awakening; about the future of our alliances; about the nature of the relationship that will exist between North America and Europe; about what sort of wider world we want to see.

What is needed now is a new concept of security rooted in universal, democratic values. What is also necessary is the genius to give constructive expression to our rediscovered sense of shared purpose. Newspaper headlines are filled with a new lexicon of diplomatic architecture—expressions such as a common European home, concentric circles, confederation, and so on. These ideas reflect the need to create new instruments of cooperation, to breathe new life into existing organizations and to bring greater definition to our common political vision of a new European future.

The new Bank for European Reconstruction and Development is one creative response to these needs. It is needed to complete the unfinished business of European economic reconstruction. The Bank will be crucial to the development of the nascent spirit of enterprise in the countries of Eastern Europe. It will also be important for the integration of the countries of Eastern Europe into the global economy. We are participating actively in this constructive and beneficial initiative and are ready to contribute time, money and expertise to aid its success.

The Conference on Security and Cooperation in Europe is, also, a vital piece of the architecture. For almost two decades, the CSCE has been an extremely important instrument for countries in both East and West; it has served as the bridge from sterile disagreement to fruitful cooperation. It has facilitated the quite extraordinary change of the past year. And it is the only institution that comprises all the countries directly engaged in European security.

A costly lesson of the history of this century is that European security and North American security are indivisible. None of us is secure when any of us feels threatened. We support the call for a summit level meeting of the CSCE later this year and believe we should begin preparations immediately. We believe we should all strive to be in a position at that summit to sign an agreement on reducing conventional forces in Europe. Further, we would like to see the CSCE transformed into an institution of ongoing economic, social and political cooperation between the countries of East and West.

In these days of torrential change and telescoped time-frames, stability and predictability in security arrangements are at a premium. For 40 years, NATO has embodied the commitment of North America to European security.

NATO, with its transatlantic membership, has a central role to play in facilitating the orderly transition from armed confrontation to more normal and productive political relationships. NATO's arms control agenda is being pursued with the same seriousness of purpose as has been applied to maintaining an appropriate military balance between East and West. And NATO provides a basis for going beyond arms issues to verification and confidence-building.

Openness is a precondition of confidence and, therefore, of stability. An agreement on Open Skies is in concert with the times; it will help to consolidate the dramatic improvement in relations between East and West that has occurred over the past year. By opening our territories to virtually unrestricted surveillance by air, we will be showing that we have nothing to hide and less to fear.

An Open Skies agreement will be a statement of enlightened political will, capitalizing on the current climate of achievement and building on a record of recent success. When this idea was first proposed in the fifties, the times were not right. Both leadership and catalytic change have ensured that the concept—a helpful, confidence-building measure—will receive fair and thoughtful consideration today. I invite all present to pursue this agreement, this time, with vision and vigour.

Quarrels and competition between East and West have had a profoundly negative influence on many areas of the world. Perhaps most significant, the Cold War distorted the functioning of the United Nations, stunted the development of multilateral cooperation and inhibited opportunities for dialogue and progress. The prospect of real peace in Europe, at last, provides us the opportunity to return to the unfinished business of building a modern and effective multilateral system.

The challenges we face as dynamic societies go well beyond orthodox definitions of national security. The global natural environment is threatened and the international institutions to protect it are inadequate. The scourge of drug abuse is felt in North and South and we have found no satisfactory collective means to curtail it. The burden of debt is prejudicing the future of middle-income countries around the world. And hunger and disease are too often the fate of the world's poorest countries mired in economic hopelessness and social despair.

This meeting in Ottawa has two main tasks. First, to concentrate diligently on the work at hand so that an agreement on Open Skies will be achieved when delegations reassemble in Budapest. And, more generally, to seize this unprecedented moment in recent history to replace the Cold War and its incalculable costs in economic wealth, misspent human genius and wasted social opportunity with a new ethic of cooperation based on peace, prosperity and common purpose.

We, who are gathered here in this room, today, bear a heavy responsibility to our nations and to history because the opportunity is given to few people to help shape a new era in world affairs. We carry the hopes and prayers of people from Vladivostok to Vancouver and from countries far removed from the old East-West axis of conflict.

Let us work, together, to multiply the gains we have made in relations between the countries of East and West. Let us dedicate ourselves to building a world that made illusory the Cold War. Let us broaden our horizons and open our skies to peace and prosperity for all. Ladies and gentlemen, the world is watching you in high expectation. Grasp the opportunity that is open to you.

On behalf of all Canadians, who are proud of your presence and grateful for your leadership, I wish you good luck.

Exchange Between President Bush and Reporters
Aboard Air Force One En Route to Toronto
About Meeting with Prime Minister Mulroney
10 April 1990

Q. What are you going to talk about?

The President. Wide array of subjects, including Europe, Central and South America, and then there are some bilateral issues. This meeting was—we talked about it for a long time, but this just seemed a wonderful way to do it. I think it's—as a baseball fan—and I think the commissioner agrees with me—this shows an interest on the part of the president, the commissioner, and the prime minister of Canada for baseball being an international sport. And as he pointed out to me, one of the biggest drawing teams in either league is the Toronto Blue Jays, and we're going to see a beautiful baseball park as well as see a good opening game for Canada. So, I think it's good. We forget sometimes they've got two very aggressive, good ball clubs in the big leagues.

Q. Don't detract from the Rangers, right?

The President. No, we don't want to detract from them at all.

Q.—call it the national pastime going to Canada?

The President. Well, I think we want to get them to buy into that definition. That's why we're going.

I want to get there the same time you guys do, so I want to put my seatbelt on.

Q. Are you going to throw a curve or a slider?

The President. I'm going to go with a slider this time. I've had such good luck in the last couple of years. The catcher let me down one time when he couldn't get into the dirt and grab it properly.

Q. See you later.

The President. I'll see you later.

Q. Are you working your stuff, Mr. President?

The President. No, no. Nolan will handle the fast one, and I'll go with the stuff.

News Conference of the President and Prime Minister
at Skydome, Toronto
10 April 1990

The Prime Minister. I just want to tell you that the president and I have had what I consider to be an excellent meeting. We'll be meeting again over dinner before the Blue Jays inflict terrible damage upon the Rangers. [Laughter] But so far, our discussions have been friendly. [Laughter] And they've touched upon East-West relations, our trade relationships, our free trade agreement, the situation in Eastern Europe, the NATO summit, the Houston summit, the results of my recent visit to Mexico and to the Caribbean and the impacts on some American policies.

We had an excellent exchange of views. We were joined by Secretary Baker and his colleagues and Mr. [Joe] Clark [Secretary of State for External Affairs] and a full Canadian delegation after, I think, the president and I had met for about an hour or so privately.

So, that, from Canada's point of view, was it. We thank you, Mr. President, for the visit of you and your colleagues. We welcome you all plus your media colleagues to Canada, and we wish you well.

The President. Well, thank you, Mr. Prime Minister. And before taking questions, let me just thank the prime minister and his colleagues for their hospitality. I can tell you that I find these talks extraordinarily helpful. We're in complicated international times.

And the relationship between Canada and the United States is strong. I, today, once again, found the three hours of talks that we had extraordinarily helpful. It is very important that Canada and the United States be on the same wavelength as much as possible.

And so, sir, I'm delighted to be here. I found that this prime minister tells it as it is, with no coloration; and I view that as extraordinarily helpful to the United States, the way a good friend, the head of a friendly country, should do. And he's very forceful. We have some differences; but most of the time, on these big issues that he was referring to, I think we have broad agreement with Canada. And I think, as we move into important talks—the G-7 [economic summit] meetings, our meeting that I'm planning to have with Mr. Gorbachev, and other meetings—it is very important that Canada and the US are together.

So, thank you, sir. I feel it's been well-worthwhile.

Lithuanian Independence

Q. Mr. President, has the stall on arms control and Moscow's tough stand in Lithuania raised questions in your mind about Mr. Gorbachev's intentions and chances for success?

The President. No. I don't know that it's raised questions about that. I think the Secretary of State made clear to Mr. Shevardnadze [Soviet Foreign Minister]—and I believe Mr. Gorbachev knows my views—that should things deteriorate regarding peaceful solution to the question of Lithuania, it would be extraordinarily difficult to move forward as rapidly as I'd like to see us move forward with them on a lot of questions. But I think on a situation that's as complicated as that one, why, you give your opinion. Our opinion is that this matter must be resolved peacefully.

We have never recognized the incorporation of Lithuania into the Soviet Union. Self-determination and freedom are hallmarks of the United States policy always. And so, be clear in talking to Mr. Gorbachev, be clear in talking to other Soviet interlocutors, and hope that they will conduct themselves in a way that can move the dramatic progress that's taken place in the last year or so even further forward.

Acid Rain

Q. Prime Minister, don't you think that you could [...talk...] with the president, on the need for the US and Canada—for an acid rain proposal?

The Prime Minister. The president, I think, is of the view that once the legislation passes the Congress—it's gone through the Senate, thanks to his leadership and the leadership of Senator Mitchell—when it gets through the House, perhaps this summer we can begin the process of negotiating a bilateral accord on acid rain, which I think would be a great tribute to what both of us have been seeking for both countries.

Lithuanian Independence

Q. Mr. President, on Lithuania and the Soviet Union, sir, you called the other day for what you called good-faith negotiations; and I wonder if you think it's really realistic to call for good-faith negotiations in an atmosphere where one side has tanks in the streets, has closed borders, and used troops to storm buildings?

The President. No, I think it's even more important to have good-faith negotiations when you have a situation of that nature. And I would just appeal to all sides and anyone with any influence to encourage dialog and discussion as a way to solve this very difficult and complicated problem, because the United States' position is clear.

Q. If I could follow up, you spoke of the need for peaceful resolutions, but I gather the administration did not comment on the specifics—as you go along here—but does the administration care about what the details of that resolution are and whether they're in any way fair to the Lithuanian side?

The President. We care because the underpinning of our policy is self-determination, freedom, and democracy.

Soviet–US Relations

Q. Mr. President, given the uncertainty about Soviet intentions in Lithuania, why did you agree to move up the dates of the summit? Doesn't that lock in the meeting and deny the United States the means of influencing the situation?

The President. No, it doesn't deny the United States the chance to do anything. I happen to believe when you have complications, that that's a good time to talk; it's a good time to have more discussion; it's a good time to avoid difficulty, if possible, and to hammer out differences. But that wasn't why the summit meeting, as I explained to the prime minister earlier, was moved up. It just happened to work out that way; and they, I think, accepted a suggestion from us within one day that was behind the scenes. So, I want to dispel the idea that because the summit came earlier than some had expected that that had something to do with turmoil out there in any place around the world. But it is very important when you have difficulties brewing that you have discussion.

The Prime Minister. To complement just on that, to complement what the president has indicated, when we were in the Soviet Union, Mr. Gorbachev made it very clear that in respect to this problem that there would be—and I think I'm quoting him—"no crackdown in regard to Lithuania." And Mr. Clark, who was there, specifically sought reassurance from Mr. Shevardnadze; and he gave Mr. Clark the reassurances that he gave to Mr. Baker as well: that that was the intention of the Soviet Union, that was the policy of the Soviet Union.

They've moved along somewhat since then. But we support the approach that—both the United States and Canada have identical positions in respect of the juridical realities of Lithuania and the manner in which it was incorporated into the Soviet Union. And so, we believe that the prudence that the president has exhibited is the proper way to go.

Canada–US Relations

Q. For the president. Sir, Canada's current constitutional problems involving Quebec—I was wondering if I could ask you, sir, whether you're concerned with the rather dramatic rise in independence feelings in Quebec and the future stability and unity...

The President. I think, rather clearly, that's a matter for Canada; and it's not a matter that would be helpful for me to involve myself in or the United States government to be involved in. It's the internal affairs of Canada. We have always enjoyed superb relations with Canada, and a unified, strong Canada is a great partner—has been, and will continue to be. But I think it would be inappropriate to comment further on a matter that is not an agenda item, nor one that I feel comfortable getting into.

Soviet President Gorbachev

Q. Mr. Prime Minister and then Mr. President as well, if I could get both your assessments on this. We've heard the president and his administration repeatedly say that their foreign policy is not based on the survival of one man in the Soviet Union—Mikhail Gorbachev. And yet in the current tension with Lithuania, we've seen that Mr. Gorbachev's survival is very important to you. Is that, in fact, the case? Is that a shift in policy? Should it be?

The President. Is this for me?

Q. Both of you, if you would.

The President. Well, I don't think you base the foreign policy of a country on any individual: you base it on what you think is right. In this case, Mr. Gorbachev, the president has a record of encouraging, or certainly acquiescing in, the peaceful evolution of democratic change in Eastern Europe—so dramatic that not one single person in this room, and you can start with me and then move briskly down the aisle here, predicted it at all.

In other words, he has demonstrated that he is committed to peaceful change and the evolution of democracy—inside, as he moves forward on *perestroika*, outside, as we see a peaceful resolution to questions in Eastern Europe that, as I say, anyone would have found difficult to predict.

But again, he is a known quantity in the West. Western interlocutors like myself—and the prime minister can speak for himself—find a frankness there and a willingness to discuss difficult problems that has not always been the case in dealing with the Soviet Union.

But again, things happen, and I don't think that the foreign policy can be shaped on the success of any individual. I mean, I think that you have to say what's right. But this man has, I think, in terms of past Soviet leaders, demonstrated an openness and a commitment to reform and openness inside that's remarkable. So, give him credit, and deal openly. But when you have difficulties like we have today, talk frankly with him about it.

The Prime Minister. On that, I was struck by the fact that when we were in Moscow, it was just at that time that the government of Czechoslovakia—I think the day before—had been overthrown. And there were 300,000 people in Wenceslas Square listening to Mr. Dubcek. And I said to him, "Well, what do you think of this?" He said, "I think it's fine; sounds good to me." And I was struck by the fact that almost 21 years earlier his predecessor's response had been to send tanks into that same square. And so, as the president says, we're dealing with an entirely different kettle of fish; and this one is more attractive and more realistic and appears to be much more in keeping with some, if not all, of the values that we in the West defend. And there has been, with some few exceptions, a great sense of leadership and the display of reasonableness that we had not come to know in earlier Soviet leaders, and that's encouraging. It's very encouraging that the dialog with President Gorbachev be maintained.

NATO

Q.—Foreign Minister Genscher [of West Germany] in Ottawa earlier suggested it was time for a redefinition of the transatlantic relationship and also a reduction in NATO. Are you and the president eye-to-eye on the long-term role for NATO and what comes after it?

The Prime Minister. Well, we're eye-to-eye on the fact that NATO and the solidarity of NATO has been responsible for preserving the peace in Europe for 50 years, and that the solidarity of NATO has been one of the key influences in bringing about the important treaties that the Soviet Union and the United States have managed to negotiate in the last four or five years, and that NATO, we believe, is an instrument for political predictability. Its existence is to the advantage both of those of us in the West and the Soviet Union. It is very important that NATO maintain its strength, but perhaps acquire a new dimension as well as the years go by.

But I don't think there's any doubt or any difference between the president and I, and we're the only two North American participants. We both have had troops in Europe since the Second World War, at great costs to both the United States and Canada. And we feel very much a part of Europe, and we want to be involved in that definition of a new architecture of Europe, as both Canada and the United States have an important role to play there. But principal, or key, to that is the solidarity of the NATO alliance.

The President. And I might add on behalf of the United States that I agree with that. And it is our responsibility to convince the Eastern Europeans, convince a unified Germany—although I hope there won't be much convincing needed—and convince the Soviet Union that the interests of stability are best served by an expanded role for NATO. Obviously, you've got different problems, different military assignments, strategy, or whatever. But here we're talking about a stable Europe, and the best answer for that is to have an expanded role for NATO. And so, I am convinced that that is the way to go, and I'm pleased that the Chancellor of Germany [Helmut Kohl of West Germany] understands that and others are beginning to understand it very, very clearly.

Q. Thank you.

North American Trade Agreement

Q. Any chance that a trilateral trade agreement with Mexico—a trilateral trade agreement for North America...

The President. Let me just say that on this one that there's no trilateral agreement being discussed. I've benefited from the debrief by Prime Minister Mulroney of a meeting that he had with President Salinas of Mexico. I will be meeting with President Salinas of Mexico. I think it is essential that Canada continue to show its extraordinary interest in matters below our border and, in this case, Mexico. And I think it is essential that the United States, interested as we are and concerned as we are about Europe, not neglect our own hemisphere. So, I learned a great deal about what I might expect when President Salinas comes to Washington by listening to Prime Minister Mulroney. But we're not talking about a trilateral agreement. We are talking about good, sound relationships between all three of these countries.

The Prime Minister. President Salinas is struck by the leadership dimensions of the Canada–US Free Trade Agreement, and I think he sees some trading relationships to be in Mexico's direct benefit. As far as Canada's concerned, while aid to developing countries is very important, we think it's even more important that developing nations be given a chance to trade their way to greater prosperity. And a free trade agreement with some of these nations may very well be something that they're going to want to consider with the United States and other trading partners.

Remarks Announcing Canada–United States Air Quality Negotiations and an Exchange With Reporters
Houston, Texas
8 July 1990

The President. Well, we're here to comment on the acid rain agreement. The joint statement that we're issuing today on beginning negotiations is long overdue. I know that this is very important for the Canadian side; and I want to say to you, sir, I appreciate your patience and understanding.

Both Houses now in the United States Congress have passed clean air bills, similar to mine, by huge margins; and the House-Senate conference will begin this week. And I think it will be of enormous benefit to both our countries. Bill Reilly, the head of the EPA, plans to be in Ottawa on July 16th and will be prepared to open preliminary discussions. We should be able to begin formal negotiations shortly after that.

And we've made great progress. And I think we ought to both be very pleased about that. Great progress has been made, but we still have a long way to go. We recognize that. And I pledge to my Canadian friends that we want to do our part, and I think this clean air legislation—that I hope I'll be able to sign soon—is but one manifestation of that.

Welcome to Houston, sir. And the floor is yours.

Prime Minister Mulroney. Thank you, Mr. President.

I'm pleased to confirm that the president and I have agreed to begin negotiations for an air quality accord. Our two countries share a long history of cooperation on transboundary environmental problems. An acid rain agreement will safeguard the natural health of our respective ecosystems, and we both fought—President Bush and I—have fought long and hard to get to where we are today.

Bill Reilly and Bob de Cotret [Canadian Minister of the Environment] will discuss this issue when they meet in Ottawa in about a week's time, and as the president has indicated, negotiations will begin shortly thereafter.

And so, we have worked hard for a bilateral accord, and I think that this day will long be remembered in the history of our relationship for the significant departure that it constitutes from past positions in regard to the environment and the protection of the environment in North America.

Joint Statement by Prime Minister Mulroney and President Bush Announcing Canada–United States Air Quality Negotiations
8 July 1990

Our two countries share a great legacy of bountiful natural resources and scenic grandeur, as well as a long history of cooperation on transboundary environmental problems. It is critical to the future well-being of Canada and the United States that we assure the continued productivity and environmental health of these natural systems: the Great Lakes and other shared water bodies, the forests, the wildlife, and the soils and farmlands.

Thus, we announce with great satisfaction that our countries have agreed to begin negotiations for a practical and effective air quality accord. US Environmental Protection Agency Administrator William K. Reilly and Canadian Environment Minister Robert de Cotret will discuss this issue when they meet in mid-July in Ottawa. We expect to begin negotiations shortly thereafter.

The initial focus of these negotiations will be on reduction of sulphur dioxide and other precursors of acid rain. With clean air legislation now before a Conference Committee of the House and Senate of the US Congress, the United States anticipates substantial progress in the years ahead in curbing acid rain and improving air quality. Since 1985 Canada has had in place its own control programme which will reduce both acid rain damage in Canada and the export of pollution to the United States. We look forward to a close working relationship between Canada and the United States to assure that our agreement on air quality and our other bilateral programmes yield tangible environmental improvements and benefits.

Remarks and a Question-and-Answer Session
With Reporters
Kennebunkport, Maine
27 August 1990

The President. Let me simply say that, once again, Prime Minister Mulroney and I have had a very good discussion—talked about bilateral matters, but also, obviously, about the situation regarding Iraq.

And Canada, a member of the Security Council, has been not only in a role of leadership there, but side by side with the United States and others. I told the Prime Minister that I'm very grateful for Canada's position. As we all know, they've contributed to this—I believe it's now 22-nation— international force, both on the land and Canada's participation on the sea—ours also—as well as land. And so, we're very grateful to them.

And once again, as I say, we've had very fruitful discussions. And prime minister, welcome back to what—when this was divined—was to be a purely social event because we want to once again welcome Brian Mulroney and his wonderful family here. But we have some of that, but we also have had an opportunity to discuss in-depth world events.

Welcome, sir, and the floor is yours until we go to the questions.

The Prime Minister. Thank you, Mr. President. We've had, and will continue a little later on, some excellent discussions, both in regard to bilateral problems which are in the process of clearing up—somewhat like the weather, although we have some important matters on our plate—but also, principally, the matter in Iraq.

I, along with all members of the government of Canada and the people of Canada, were pleased—very pleased—with the decision of the United Nations Security Council to provide what I believe is quite unprecedented leadership. Certainly one of the most important days of the United Nations since its foundation have been the series of resolutions in respect of Iraq, where the United Nations as one—Security Council—dealt effectively and well with a rogue leader who sought to annex another nation and believed that he could conduct himself with impunity, both vis-à-vis his Arab neighbours and the world.

And the world turned against him in a quite extraordinary manner. And that is to the credit of the United Nations and those who—pursuant to the lead of the United States under President Bush—like-minded nations who participated in what we believe is a very important initiative to curb aggression in the Middle East.

And so, I'm happy to have this opportunity to review some very important matters with the president, thank him again for his hospitality. And I would be happy to take whatever questions come my way.

Persian Gulf Crisis

Q. Prime Minister, if I could start by asking you whether there was some discussion of the conditions under which Canada's military presence in the Middle East might be enlarged?

The Prime Minister. No. We believe that our contribution for the moment is adequate, but as the Minister of Defence has indicated in the past, we haven't ruled out or ruled in anything else either. We are firmly resolved to resist the aggression and to join with our friends and allies in pursuit of that objective. But we seek, obviously, a peaceful resolution of this; and we're very pleased with the initiatives that may hold some promise from the Secretary General of the United Nations. And the president and I have had an opportunity to touch on that briefly.

Q. Mr. President, aren't you concerned, by the action that you took today against the Iraqi Embassy [expulsion of Iraqi diplomats from the United States], that you're increasing the tension and lessening the possibilities for a diplomatic solution and you're also possibly giving the Iraqis more of a rationale to take harsher action against our own diplomats and the hostages?

The President. No, I'm not concerned about that at all. This is an action that others are taking. Nobody will be held against their will. They're all free to go. In essence, we're kind of keeping some reasonable parallelism in terms of numbers. So, I don't think there's any chance for any misunderstanding on that account.

Q. Can I ask you, just to follow up, Mr. President: You said a couple of weeks ago that you didn't really see much prospect at the time for a diplomatic solution. Has that changed? Do you see more hope now?

The President. Well, I don't particularly see more hope now because it's so clear what the world is demanding of Saddam Hussein [President of Iraq]. Clearly the objectives remain the same: get out of Kuwait and restore the rightful leaders to their place. But the Secretary General, I understand, will be meeting with Foreign Minister of Iraq [Tariq Aziz]—I think it's in Amman, Jordan. I haven't talked to him yet. I have a call in to him and will probably get him. But the UN mandate is so clear and, on the other hand, Saddam Hussein has been so resistant to complying with international law that I don't yet see fruitful negotiations.

But the Secretary General, knowing the UN mandate, is a very good man. And I might add, parenthetically, the prime minister and I both did talk about this, and we both agree that the UN has perhaps demonstrated its finest in recent actions. So, if Perez de Cuellar, an old friend of mine, wants to go forward and try to find some way to get the UN action complied with, so much the better.

Q. Mr. Prime Minister, in light of the US decision today, would Canada consider similar action in expelling Iraqi diplomats or nationals from Canada or taking any sort of action against them?

The Prime Minister. We are going to—this is a time-honoured diplomatic practice, and if it applies to Canada, we won't hesitate to take remedial action. What you have is an abuse of—one of the most fundamental privileges of democratic and civilized nations is, namely, to be represented in another's country without our representatives being harassed or intimidated or assaulted. Those assaults can take place in many ways, and we have to make sure that the fundamental rule of international law is respected. So, if there is a requirement for us to do so in Canada with our own ambassadors and our own representatives, we will exercise reciprocity.

Q. Mr. President, do you have any assurances or will you seek any assurances from Perez de Cuellar not to try to negotiate something beyond the UN sanctions—cut a deal that may undercut the sanctions themselves?

The President. It's inconceivable to me that the Secretary General, an experienced diplomat, a good leader, would do that. I think it would be gratuitous for me to discuss that with him. He knows what the United Nations has done. He knows how unanimous the support has been for resolution after resolution. So, it's inconceivable to me that he would not have that message. He's a very sound man. Actually, as Brian Mulroney reminded me, he had a very useful role, I believe, in between Iran and Iraq. But, no, I wouldn't give any gratuitous advice of that nature. It's so clear; it's so obvious.

Q. Is there a danger once you go down this path of negotiations on one day and small peace offerings the next that this thing could be dragged out and world resolve will crumble?

The President. No. I've never seen the world community so closely aligned against this man. Somebody asked me the other day at a press conference here—Saddam Hussein said he'd like to talk. We have a Chargé there... He could go talk to him, have his people talk to him.

So, I'm not saying we're not going to talk. But what, clearly, world opinion is saying and what the United Nations has said and what is now codified in international law is: Out, Saddam Hussein, Iraqi, out of Kuwait, and restore the leaders! But you have to talk to get there. But that doesn't mean there is to be compromise. Clearly, we would oppose any compromise on these fundamental principles that have been laid down by the United Nations.

Persian Gulf Conflict

Q. Mr. President, President Gorbachev of the Soviet Union called on Arabs today to display their ability to consolidate very quickly to increase their presence in this conflict to avoid actual armed confrontation. He said it would be necessary for them to do that. Do you agree with that? Is the first question—do you agree that they have to interject themselves more forcefully into this?

The President. I think the Arab world has been responsibly united in opposition to Saddam Hussein's aggression. I did not see that particular comment by President Gorbachev; but since you've invoked his name, let me simply say I've been very pleased with the way the Soviets, for their part, have conducted themselves at the United Nations and elsewhere. But I didn't see that, so I can't comment. But I would simply say that I think both the prime minister and I are very pleased that a number of Arab countries have joined in the position that we've talked about here. And indeed, it's only a tiny minority that is in opposition.

And so, I keep coming back—it is not as Saddam Hussein is trying to make it: the Arab world against the United States. It is the United States and most of the Arab world and Canada and other countries against this outrageous aggression. We've got to keep saying that so there will be no erosion—the erosion that Jim [Jim Miklaszewski, NBC News] asked about. But it's true, and everyone knows it's true.

Q. Have you talked with President Gorbachev or do you plan to, if not?

The President. I haven't talked to him recently. As you know, the Secretary of State has been in very close contact with [Soviet] Foreign Minister Shevardnadze.

Q. Mr. Mulroney, can you say exactly how many Canadians are trapped in Iraq and Kuwait, and why you won't call them hostages, as George Bush does?

The Prime Minister. Well, I've indicated that President Bush has information and circumstances that quite appropriately allow him to describe American citizens held the way they are in the manner in which he has. There are large numbers of Canadian nationals being held—I think the third largest number of foreigners held in Kuwait and in and around Baghdad. And we have not yet [received] the kind of information that would allow me to apply that word to the Canadian citizens being detained. Which is not to suggest that it couldn't happen tomorrow, and it certainly is not to suggest that it shouldn't have happened at all.

It's quite an achievement when a leader of a state in 1990 can make himself a pariah not only with leaders around the world but with his immediate Arab neighbours. That's quite a piece of work to be able to do that all in a short period of time. And to provoke what is an extraordinary response of leadership by the United Nations and the allies in such a short period of time is in itself another good piece of work—among the finest in the United Nations since its foundation.

Persian Gulf Crisis

Q. Mr. President, how would you describe your policy for ousting Saddam Hussein right now, as of this moment? Would it be fair to describe it as wait and see?

The President. No. My policy is to do everything we can, working with other nations, to enforce the sanctions. We have moved forces, considerable forces, and I hope that that has safeguarded Saudi Arabia, which in my view was clearly threatened when Saddam Hussein moved his forces south from Kuwait City. So, I think it is now: get plenty of force in place—we're still doing that. Enforce the United Nations sanctions rigorously—and for the US, we will do that and encourage others to do it. And that's about where we are right now.

Q. You were very effective, sir, in getting the UN to join in on this sea blockade. Are you now considering doing the same thing on an air interdiction policy?

The President. Well, I don't think there have been many examples of this net being penetrated, broken through, by air. But we have been talking to countries about not permitting over-flight and tightening up in every way, all aspects of the economic sanctions that were called for by the United Nations.

Q. Prime Minister, have you discussed, the two of you, under what circumstances Canada could play a larger role in this? And, Mr. President, would you welcome a larger Canadian role?

The Prime Minister. We haven't discussed it, but I've indicated earlier that Canada hasn't added anything in or added it out. We will play it as circumstances develop. We think that our contribution is appropriate. As I said when I announced it, Canada is not a superpower. But we believe that we—along with countries, for example, all the way to Australia—have an obligation to stand with our friends and allies and resist aggression. And if more is required, the Government of Canada will consider that and make an appropriate decision. But for the moment, we're pleased with the leadership of the United Nations, very pleased with the skill of the president of the United States and the manner in which he has brought about quite a remarkable display of solidarity, both from our European partners and around the world.

I think that the achievement of the president, if I may say, in respect to the Arab world is certainly unprecedented in my memory. That this kind of action would be contemplated with the results of approval coming as strongly as they have from so many Arab nations is in itself a remarkable achievement of political leadership, and I think it's important to note that.

Q. This is really a question for both of you, sir. For all this talk of unanimity, there seems to be divergences on tactics. You are content to use force. The Soviets say they won't use force to stop the blockade. You have hostages; Prime Minister Mulroney does not have hostages. Mrs. Thatcher doesn't think talking is such a good idea. Is there a divergence, and is it potentially undermining?

The President. I think any nuances of difference are so overwhelmed by the common ground that they are almost meaningless, is the way I view it. I mean, I think the thing of note is how together everybody is, not that there might be nuances of difference.

The Prime Minister. Well, I've noticed the points that you make. If somebody had told you two years ago that this kind of crisis would emerge and the Soviet Union would repudiate Iraq and that the United Nations Security Council would stand in unanimous support of five resolutions and that you would see this kind of support emerge, as I say, from Canada to Australia, you would have bought him a ticket to the funny farm right away.

This is a historic achievement by the United Nations, by members of the alliance, and by the president of the United States. This is a remarkable achievement. There are few parallels for it, certainly, in modern history. But there are differences of opinion. Sure there are. You better believe it; they happen all the time. The story is not that. It's that there are so few of them and so modest in nature, given the profound dimensions of the challenge. There will be others ahead of us, and it's going to require this kind of cooperation and consultation to make sure that they all mesh together and that we try and bring about the end that is sought.

Q. Mr. President, if Saddam Hussein is in a box, as General Scowcroft [Assistant to the President for National Security Affairs] said yesterday, are you willing to give him any way out, short of unconditional surrender? Which is to say, if there are going to be negotiations, what's negotiable here?

The President. Well, certainly not the UN position. The position of the international law is not negotiable. I think that's what Prime Minister Thatcher was addressing herself to. I would agree with that. The United Nations has spoken—country after country supporting the action taken by the Security Council. So, there's no room for compromise or negotiation on that point. But I don't think you should ever say you'll never talk about anything. But I'm not saying that there's any flexibility, is what your question is. And there is no flexibility on Iraq getting out of Kuwait and the rulers being permitted to come back to Kuwait.

Q. But is there any flexibility on the future composition of the Kuwait Government, which is to say...

The President. No.

Notes for a Statement on the Persian Gulf Crisis
Prime Minister Brian Mulroney
Ottawa
14 September 1990

On 2 August, with neither provocation or warning, one member of the United Nations—Iraq—invaded and occupied another smaller, member—Kuwait—. The government of Kuwait fled into exile.

In the face of Iraq's naked aggression, and with Iraq's armed forces in a position to strike swiftly into Saudi Arabia, the government of Kuwait and the government of Saudi Arabia sought the assistance of the world community.

Subsequently, Iraq has detained innocent foreigners, including Canadians. Iraqi forces have cruelly driven tens of thousands of Third World guest workers out of Kuwait and Iraq—with no consideration for their welfare and indeed, for their survival.

And the Iraqi leader has sought to sow insurrection among the populations of neighbouring Arab states and to incite animosity between Christians and Moslems. But this is not a conflict between Arabs and the West or between Iraq and the United States. It is Saddam Hussein against the World.

The UN Security Council, in a performance of historic importance, has adopted five resolutions condemning the Iraqi invasion and calling on members of the UN to take action, including imposing comprehensive economic sanctions. The UN is responding to this crisis in the way that the architects of the UN—with the experience of two world wars behind them—envisaged it would respond in such circumstances.

Today, 25 countries, including nine Arab nations, have stationed military forces in the Gulf region. Rarely has the world community been so united in the face of aggression. Never has the UN responded more effectively. And not in 40 years has the case for Canadian action been clearer or more compelling.

As a member of the UN, and as a country with a fundamental interest in the preservation of the rule of international law, Canada has played a leading role on this issue—diplomatically, at the United Nations, and in the protection of Canadians in Kuwait and Iraq; militarily, with our despatch of the Canadian forces; economically, in respecting the economic sanctions against Iraq; and, humanely, in assisting the effort to help the tens of thousands of peoples stranded in the desert.

My cabinet colleagues and I have just had a thorough discussion of the situation in the Gulf and of Canada's response to it. In the course of those discussions, we have come to a number of decisions. First, we have decided, to place the crews of the *Athabaskan*, the *Terra Nova* and the *Protecteur* on active service for this operation as of tomorrow, 15 September.

The Governor General will be asked to sign the requisite Order-in-Council tomorrow. We will table the Order-in-Council when the House resumes 24 September, thereby respecting Canadian Parliamentary tradition. And the issue will be debated by Parliament. You will recall that we had decided in August not to give the ships' crews their final mission tasking because we wanted to take into account the latest developments internationally before we fully defined their mission.

Subsequent UN resolutions, particularly resolution 665, confirmed the wisdom of our initial position and helped us to define the ships' mission. The task that our forces are being given is to cooperate with other, like-minded countries in deterring further Iraqi aggression and in ensuring strict implementation of the economic sanctions laid down in UN Security Council resolution 661 whose objective, among other things, is to end Iraq's occupation of Kuwait.

We have, further, decided to accept the advice of our military staff to have our ships operate within the Persian Gulf. They will be under Canadian command and control and will have responsibility for a sector across the middle of the Gulf, north of the Strait of Hormuz and south of Bahrain.

Our ships will be operating in the same general area as the ships of the US and the UK and other, European navies. This decision, taken after consultations among contributing navies, is based on military considerations.

The Canadian ships will be able to play a meaningful role operationally in that sector and will benefit from the advanced air defence capabilities of the US and UK forces. Of course, the ships also have their own, recently upgraded air defence capability. We have further decided to deploy a squadron of 12–18 CF18 fighter aircraft to the Gulf to provide air cover for our ships under Canadian control.

The Iraqi invasion of Kuwait has spawned terrible human misery. We have already contributed $2.5 million to international relief agencies to assist displaced people. We have decided this morning to double our contribution.

We have decided, as well, to lease transport aircraft to help convey third world refugees to their home countries. We will, also, airlift third world country ground forces to Saudi Arabia.

On return to their homelands, the displaced citizens of the poorer countries will still face an uncertain future, because their own governments cannot afford to handle such an influx. We have decided, therefore, to increase our development assistance funds earmarked for Sri Lanka, the Philippines and Bangladesh [by up to $10 million]. Three countries whose cooperation is vital to the effective functioning of the sanctions against Iraq —Turkey, Jordan and Egypt—are carrying a disproportionate burden in the Gulf.

At the same time they have, themselves, suffered severe economic setbacks as a side-effect of the sanctions and from assisting tens of thousands of displaced people. We have, therefore, decided to contribute [$30] million to help these countries. Canada's non-military financial contribution will total between [$50 and $60] million.

Taken together with our military commitments, Canada's response to the crisis in the Persian Gulf is a substantial and effective contribution to the preservation of international law and the upholding of international order.

Chapter 3:

Like Ugly on an Ape: Combatting North American Acid Rain

1991

Introduction

If the partnership between Bush and Mulroney had a single highlight for 1991, it might simply be summed up as "acid rain." In March of that year, fresh from his successful leadership of the coalition that won the Gulf War for the United Nations, Bush again visited the Canadian capital to sign the historic accord. Though it might have been cold outside in Ottawa's winter winds, it was anything but during a special ceremony on Parliament Hill. On 13 March 1991, Bush and Mulroney affixed their signatures to the long sought (and fought for) treaty designed to combat acid rain on both sides of the border.

For Mulroney, who had been championing the battle against this environmental scourge since his first meeting as leader of the Opposition with President Ronald Reagan in June of 1984, it was a particularly proud moment in his nine-year premiership. Americans were winners as well, and the success of the day—and the long-term success of the treaty itself— was put best by Bush during his speech in Ottawa at the special ceremony. "They (Canadians) were on us like ugly on an ape," he said. "The fact that Canada and the US were able so quickly to craft a wide ranging and effective agreement on such a complex subject says a lot about the extraordinary relations of our two countries… And I think we're doing something good and decent today."

In his 2007 *Memoirs*, Mulroney himself examined the legacy both men left in their wake in this area on the North American environment. "What has happened in the 16 years since?" he asked. "According to a study by the nonpartisan Library of Parliament in August 2004, total Canadian sulphur dioxide emissions were 20 per cent lower than Canada's agreed-upon national cap and 45 per cent below the 1980 baseline level. In the United States, sulphur dioxide emissions had dropped by 32 per cent from the 1990 level and were down a total of 35 percent from the 1980 level."[14]

It was not "all work and no play" for the two good-natured leaders during their four years together, of course. Early in his presidency, Bush established the Brent Scowcroft Award for Somnolent Excellence—a tongue-in-cheek commendation granted by the president to high-ranking officials (foreign and US) who fell asleep at important meetings. Improbably, the prime minister himself mounted an involuntary challenge for the Scowcroft Award during a pivotal NATO meeting.

"I had flown through the night to be there," Mulroney recalled, "but I can't sleep on planes, even though I tried to go to bed in the bedroom. Anyway, when we arrived in Brussels, I was very tired. My foreign secretary, Barbara McDougall, had come in from Japan in the meantime, and she was also extremely tired. So we started the meetings in the morning, and after lunch they were still droning on, and on, and on—and I found myself having to move my mouth around just to stay awake. At that particular moment, I looked straight across the room, and President Bush, along with Jim Baker and (chief of staff John) Sununu, were watching me closely—knowing my predicament. The next thing I know, a Secret Service agent tapped me on the shoulder and said, "Prime Minister, I have a message for you from the president of the United States." I thanked him, and opened the paper. It read: "Brian, please protect and do not show to your foreign minister under pain of death. You have heard of the prestigious Scowcroft Award awarded annually for that person who falls asleep during meetings and does it with the most style. Recovery counts, duration counts, and style counts… Last year Iceland and Japan waged a shootout at CSCE [Commission on Security and Cooperation in Europe]. Iceland won it. Their PM and foreign minister both zonked out—totally—during the Italian speech. It might interest you to know that Barbara McDougall has challenged today, but—too bad—it was but a modest effort. 'Style' OK, but 'duration' spotty. On 'recovery' she did very well, smiling, a good show. PS: It is unlikely she will win because her challenge was sporadic."

On the world stage, both leaders continued to grapple with the challenges presented by the imploding Soviet empire, which culminated in August of 1991 with a last-gasp coup by hard-liners against Mikhail Gorbachev. At the time, the media had greeted the initial reports of the coup as an "intelligence failure" and laid the blame squarely at Bush's door. Meanwhile, behind the scenes, the two leaders discussed the possible fallout should the plotters succeed.

---

14   Mulroney. see *Memoirs*. p 841.

"George," Mulroney said the morning the news broke, "one point where you may get some criticism on behalf of all of us: They may say, well, if you people had been more generous in London [at the G-7 economic summit Gorbachev had also attended seeking massive financial assistance from the West], maybe this wouldn't have happened."

"I'll get hit for holding the country to close to Gorbachev," Bush responded, but also insisted that if he did receive such attacks, "I'll point out it's a damn good thing because look at the changes that have taken place, and, if we had tried to pull out the rug, it [the coup] would have happened sooner."[15]

On Christmas Day 1991, a composed Mikhail Gorbachev prepared to hand the reins of power to Boris Yeltsin, and placed some of his final phone calls from the Kremlin to his counterparts Bush and Mulroney. He thanked both leaders for their constructive leadership in the evolution of his country and the world, assured them of the safely of the former empire's nuclear force in the days ahead, and prepared to enter history both proudly and with the thanks of his nation's former foes.

That night, with but a handful of passersby walking through Red Square, the red sickle and hammer of the Soviet standard was drawn down from the Kremlin ramparts, replaced by the three broad and bright stripes of the new Russian Federation. The Cold War was over. Freedom had finally prevailed. A new, more hopeful, yet challenging chapter in humanity was about to dawn.

James McGrath and Arthur Milnes

---

15   Bush and Scowcroft. see *A World Transformed*. p 522.

Joint Statement Announcing Canada–Mexico–United States Trilateral Free Trade Negotiations
5 February 1991

The President of the United States, George Bush; the President of the United Mexican States, Carlos Salinas de Gortari; and the Prime Minister of Canada, Brian Mulroney, announced today their intention to pursue a North American free trade agreement creating one of the world's largest liberalized markets.

Following consultations among their ministers responsible for international trade, the three leaders concluded that a North American free trade agreement would foster sustained economic growth through expanded trade and investment in a market comprising over 360 million people and trillion in output. In so doing, the agreement would help all three countries meet the economic challenges they will face over the next decade.

Accordingly, the three leaders have agreed that their trade ministers should proceed as soon as possible, in accordance with each country's domestic procedures, with trilateral negotiations aimed at a comprehensive North American free trade agreement. The goal would be to progressively eliminate obstacles to the flow of goods and services and to investment, provide for the protection of intellectual property rights, and establish a fair and expeditious dispute settlement mechanism.

President George H.W. Bush
Address to the Nation on the Suspension of
Allied Offensive Combat Operations in the Persian Gulf
Oval Office, Washington
27 February 1991

Kuwait is liberated. Iraq's army is defeated. Our military objectives are met. Kuwait is once more in the hands of Kuwaitis, in control of their own destiny. We share in their joy, a joy tempered only by our compassion for their ordeal.

Tonight the Kuwaiti flag once again flies above the capital of a free and sovereign nation. And the American flag flies above our Embassy.

Seven months ago, America and the world drew a line in the sand. We declared that the aggression against Kuwait would not stand. And tonight, America and the world have kept their word.

This is not a time of euphoria, certainly not a time to gloat. But it is a time of pride: pride in our troops; pride in the friends who stood with us in the crisis; pride in our nation and the people whose strength and resolve made victory quick, decisive, and just. And soon we will open wide our arms to welcome back home to America our magnificent fighting forces.

No one country can claim this victory as its own. It was not only a victory for Kuwait but a victory for all the coalition partners. This is a victory for the United Nations, for all mankind, for the rule of law, and for what is right.

After consulting with Secretary of Defense Cheney, the Chairman of the Joint Chiefs of Staff, General Powell, and our coalition partners, I am pleased to announce that at midnight tonight eastern standard time, exactly 100 hours since ground operations commenced and six weeks since the start of Desert Storm, all United States and coalition forces will suspend offensive combat operations. It is up to Iraq whether this suspension on the part of the coalition becomes a permanent cease-fire.

Coalition political and military terms for a formal cease-fire include the following requirements:

Iraq must release immediately all coalition prisoners of war, third country nationals, and the remains of all who have fallen. Iraq must release all Kuwaiti detainees. Iraq also must inform Kuwaiti authorities of the location and nature of all land and sea mines. Iraq must comply fully with all relevant United Nations Security Council resolutions. This includes a rescinding of Iraq's August decision to annex Kuwait and acceptance in principle of Iraq's responsibility to pay compensation for the loss, damage, and injury its aggression has caused.

The coalition calls upon the Iraqi Government to designate military commanders to meet within 48 hours with their coalition counterparts at a place in the theatre of operations to be specified to arrange for military aspects of the cease-fire. Further, I have asked Secretary of State Baker to request that the United Nations Security Council meet to formulate the necessary arrangements for this war to be ended.

This suspension of offensive combat operations is contingent upon Iraq's not firing upon any coalition forces and not launching Scud missiles against any other country. If Iraq violates these terms, coalition forces will be free to resume military operations.

At every opportunity, I have said to the people of Iraq that our quarrel was not with them but instead with their leadership and, above all, with Saddam Hussein. This remains the case. You, the people of Iraq, are not our enemy. We do not seek your destruction. We have treated your POWs with kindness. Coalition forces fought this war only as a last resort and look forward to the day when Iraq is led by people prepared to live in peace with their neighbors.

We must now begin to look beyond victory and war. We must meet the challenge of securing the peace. In the future, as before, we will consult with our coalition partners. We've already done a good deal of thinking and planning for the postwar period, and Secretary Baker has already begun to consult with our coalition partners on the region's challenges. There can be, and will be, no solely American answer to all these challenges. But we can assist and support the countries of the region and be a catalyst for peace. In this spirit, Secretary Baker will go to the region next week to begin a new round of consultations.

This war is now behind us. Ahead of us is the difficult task of securing a potentially historic peace. Tonight though, let us be proud of what we have accomplished. Let us give thanks to those who risked their lives. Let us never forget those who gave their lives. May God bless our valiant military forces and their families, and let us all remember them in our prayers.

Remarks by the President and Prime Minister at the Air Quality Agreement Signing Ceremony, Ottawa
3 March 1991

The Prime Minister. Mr. President, distinguished guests: I'm very pleased to welcome President Bush to Canada on his first foreign trip since the end of the Gulf war. He comes to Canada today as a president who is greatly admired at home and widely respected abroad, and one whose skill and resolve provided the international community with a stunning success in a war over Iraq.

In my many meetings and conversations with President Bush since August 2nd, I have been struck both by his grasp of the issues and by the breadth of his vision in regard to this remarkable problem. He instinctively chose to work within the United Nations. He painstakingly constructed and nurtured a great and disparate coalition of sovereign nations. He provided the perspective and the patience required for successful statecraft. And when, at the 11th hour, a diplomatic solution was again rejected, President Bush provided the strength and the decisiveness required for the successful prosecution of war.

I'm not entirely certain how history will interpret the expression "defining moment," which appears to be pretty much *en vogue* in certain quarters these days, but I assume it means the crystallization of great need and wise, confident leadership in a manner that indelibly affects succeeding generations. In that regard, the conduct of the Gulf crisis and the war, from its uncertain beginnings to its triumphant end, was in fact, a defining moment for the United Nations, the United States, and the world. And for this extraordinary achievement the name George Bush will live proudly in the history of free men and women.

In fact, this presidency, in my judgement, will always be remembered for the uncommon courage and the strong leadership that President George Bush of the United States of America demonstrated throughout an exceptionally challenging and potentially explosive period in world history.

Canada and the United States are close friends and trusted allies. And the president of the United States is always most welcome in our country. And, Mr. President, I bid you, on behalf of everyone, a most warm welcome here today...

It's a particular pleasure for us to welcome you, Mr. President, on this visit to sign the Canada–United States Air Quality Accord. This agreement has had a long and sometimes difficult history. It has involved three United States administrations and five successive Canadian governments. You and I, Mr. President, have worked on this issue since the days when you were still vice president. And I see Allan Gotlieb here today—when Allan was our ambassador in the United States, and so many others who have played an important role in it. But no one has played a more critical role than you.

You have demonstrated sensitivity to Canadian interests in your proceeding with domestic clean air legislation and in signing this agreement today. It commits the governments of both countries, this arrangement today, to a series of targets and schedules, and requires both to make public the progress that is achieved. The agreement also provides a framework for cooperation to solve other trans-boundary air pollution problems...

With this agreement and with the control programmes now in effect in both countries, we are confident that the acid rain menace will be eliminated by the year 2000.

I would like to take this opportunity—there are many people who deserve to be thanked today. Davie Fulton from the IJC, and I mentioned Allan. And so many others: John Fraser, who is the Speaker of the House of Commons, Mr. President, but in his previous incarnation was Minister of the Environment, and a most successful one. And I see Bill Reilly, who is here from the United States; and Robert de Cotret; and David MacDonald, who is Chairman of the Environment Committee of the House of Commons; and so many parliamentarians who are with us today who played a key role.

But I would like to thank Michael Phillips, of External Affairs, and Bob Slater, of Environment Canada, our negotiators, for a job well done. And I would like to thank their American counterparts and the scores of people on both sides, many of whom are present this afternoon, for working so hard to make this happy day possible.

Mr. President, this agreement is very important to Canadians. Our national soul takes its breath from the forests and lakes and mountains and prairies that give life to our country. The Aboriginal peoples of Canada have taught us that we hold this magnificent land, as you do yours, in trust for future generations. And so, today's agreement will help us correct many of the errors of the past.

With this agreement we are guaranteeing our children that air quality will never again be taken for granted on this continent. The sensitivity and idealism of children on both sides of the border are our environment's best hope.

Mr. President, your colleagues from the administration, Governor Sununu and General Scowcroft, and your colleagues, Ambassador Ney: on behalf of Canadians young and old, I would like to express our appreciation for your cooperation.

There is someone here, Stan Darling, Mr. President, who is right over there, who, as he says, is a member of the Conservative Caucus, soon to be 80 years young, as he says every Wednesday [caucus day for the parties on Parliament Hill in Ottawa]. He was one of the often unmentioned guiding lights who fought the fight over many long and difficult years to make this possible. And while you and I get to sign it today, Mr. President, what we sign is a tribute to Stan Darling and so many members of Parliament and members of Congress and members of the administration on both sides who deserve this tribute today.

So, I would like to express our appreciation for your cooperation, and I want to thank you for your vital contribution to preserving the common environment we both hold in trust for future generations. I'm aware, Mr. President, of the pressures on you. There are actually some pressures on us in the same ways up here in Canada. And to have moved, as you did, the environmental question so quickly within your own borders, so far and to such heights, is a tribute to the commitment that you made to the American people and to the Government of Canada—that if elected, you would make this your highest priority and you would try to bring about a day like today. Well, we're here, Mr. President, and we're here on a happy day in very large measure because you provided that principal leadership. You followed through when you gave your commitment. And for that and many other reasons I express our thanks. And I give you the warmest of welcomes to Canada.

Minister de Cotret. President Bush has certainly demonstrated an unprecedented interest in the bilateral environment affairs of Canada and the United States. Mr. President, Canadians look forward to making further improvements to our shared heritage. Allow me to add my appreciation to that of the prime minister. Ladies and gentlemen, the president of the United States.

The President. Thank you all very much for that welcome to Canada. And, Mr. Prime Minister, it's a delight to be with you and Mrs. Mulroney again. And to Minister de Cotret, why, thank you, sir, for presiding at this historic occasion, one that we've been looking forward to very, very much.

To the Members of the Parliament and to our able Ambassador, Eddie Ney, it's a great pleasure to be up here and then to add my name along with our country's commitment to an agreement of great environmental importance. I, too, would like to pay my respects to Mr. Darling. I can't say I have felt his lash or his determination as much as others in this Parliament have felt—[laughter]—but I would like to assure him that while he was fighting the domestic battles here, sensitizing Canadians—and sometimes it spilled over to sensitizing those south of the border here—Ambassadors Gotlieb and Burney were no paper tigers. They were on us like ugly on an ape, I'll tell you. [Laughter] And they stayed on us, and appropriately so, because, I think because of their leadership, they had brought many in the United States Congress and many in the administration to understand just how important a priority this was to the prime minister and to the members here. And so, I salute them as well.

Before I speak about this agreement briefly, let me just make a brief comment to underscore my sincere appreciation for the key contribution made by your country to the coalition's recent victory in the war to liberate Kuwait. Mr. Prime Minister, since the very first minute that you and I talked, Canada and the United States were appropriately, significantly side by side. And I thank you, sir, I thank the Canadian people, I thank the Members of this Parliament for standing in partnership for the principles that gave justice real meaning in the world. I once again want to say that I would talk—I'm sure it seemed to him endlessly—but to your prime minister, and the American people knew from day one exactly where Canada stood. And we are very, very grateful for that.

This agreement that we're fixing to sign is added proof that the challenges we face require a new partnership among nations. Last year at the Houston economic summit, we agreed to give this effort real priority. Our negotiators gained momentum with the passage in the US of our landmark environmental legislation, the *Clean Air Act* of 1990. Credit for this accord belongs to the EPA in our country, its able Administrator, Bill Reilly, who is with us today. And of course, credit goes to the negotiators on both sides for the spirit in which they completed this task. Let me thank our special negotiator, Dick Smith, and his colleagues, as well as their counterparts across the table on the Canadian side for a job well done.

Beyond our common interest in our shared environment, this agreement says something about our overall relationship. The fact that Canada and the United States were able so quickly to craft a wide-ranging and effective agreement on such a complex subject says a lot about the extraordinarily strong relationship between our two countries.

Mr. Prime Minister, I do recall our own discussions on environmental issues, and especially our meeting before I became president back in January of 1987. I made a comment then that made its way into more than a few Canadian news reports, that I'd gotten "an earful" from you on acid rain. That was the understatement of the year. [Laughter] So now, I came up here to prove to you that I was listening, and all of us on the American side were listening. And again, we appreciate your strong advocacy, your articulate advocacy of this principle that I think will benefit the American people, the Canadian people. And I like to think it goes even beyond the borders of our two great countries.

So, thank you very much. The treaty that we sign today is testimony to the seriousness with which both our countries regard this critical environmental issue. And here is one that did take two to tango. Here is one where each had to come give a little and take a little, and it's been worth it. And I think we're doing something good and sound and decent today.

President's News Conference With
Prime Minister Brian Mulroney of Canada
Ottawa
13 March 1991

The Prime Minister. The president and I had an opportunity for slightly over an hour so far to review both some bilateral relationships and problems that we do have in the trade area and elsewhere, but also to begin the process of discussing the evolving situation in the Middle East.

As you know, Secretary of External Affairs Joe Clark is returning tonight to join us at dinner after an extensive trip throughout the Middle East. He left Tehran earlier today and will be back, and we look forward to pursuing these questions later on tonight.

Arms Control

Q. Mr. President, as you know, our prime minister has proposed a global arms summit under the UN auspices to stop the spread of both conventional and nonconventional weapons. I was wondering, sir, if you could tell us whether you endorse that mechanism as a way of tackling this problem.

The President. One of the goals that I spelled out, one of the points I made in my speech to our Congress, was the need to do something about the proliferation of weapons. I'll have a chance to talk to Prime Minister Mulroney about that. I'm not sure exactly what the proper structure is, but clearly, that idea might have some merit. But again, it's a little early. He has not asked me to endorse that proposal, and again, I would like to talk to him before I commit ourselves further on it.

But the idea of coming together in a multilateral way to do something about the proliferation of weapons into the Middle East is something that has some appeal to me. We've seen multilateral diplomacy try and, in some ways, be effective in the Middle East, and I don't want to forget that. I don't want to start going it alone, and I don't think Canada wants to start going it alone.

Middle East Peace Process

Q. Thank you, Mr. President. I would like to ask you about Secretary Baker's trip to the Middle East. Do you see any sign that Israeli or Palestinian leaders are willing to make any kind of fundamental change in their long-held positions?

The President. Well, I would say this... the reports—and I've gotten a report every night, each night, from Jim Baker, and then Brent Scowcroft has been, I think, even in more touch with him. I think that the Secretary feels that the climate is now better than it's been in a long time for making progress.

I can't tell you about radically shifting positions, but it is my view that we ought to move forward. I think the United States is in as good a position, if not better position, than it has ever been to be a catalyst for peace there.

Put it this way—let me rephrase it—I haven't seen anything pessimistic coming out of the Baker reports. I've not had the report since he's been into Syria. But up until then, I was fully informed, and I think the mood is that we have a chance now. But that's as far as I would want to go.

Q. There is no sign of any change, real change, on either side?

The President. I think to say what I just said, you'd have to assume that there is some kind of change. I think it's fair to say there's some kind of change. The threat to some of the countries in the region is clearly down—the threat from Iraq, which has been a major threat to several countries there. And that in itself is significant change and offers a better potential for peaceful arrangement.

The Prime Minister. Perhaps I could just add a word to that. One of the reports that we've been getting from Secretary Clark, who has been a little ahead of Secretary Baker in some of the areas, has been the resounding reaction he has received from Arab leaders, most recently in Damascus yesterday, of the degree to which they were impressed by the solidarity of the coalition and the leadership of the United States in the war.

They have conveyed to Mr. Clark, all of them, the extent to which they were impressed with the fact that the coalition went so far to defend an Arab country under siege. This has registered very, very deeply, and I think has placed the membership of the coalition, and in particular the United States, in a particularly—as Mr. Clark says—a particularly advantageous position to take advantage of what he thinks are new and perhaps important opportunities there.

Canadian Unity

Q. Mr. President, have you and the prime minister had a chance yet, or will you discuss the national unity crisis in Canada, which has worsened significantly since your last visit here? And how do you regard the prospect of an independent Quebec and a fractured Canada on your northern border?

The President. I would, on that question—we barely touched on the question, to answer the first part of your question.

Secondly, I would say that the United States, for many years, has enjoyed the best possible relations with a unified Canada. I am not about to come up here and intervene into the internal affairs of Canada. But I can say from Canada's biggest trading partner and Canada's staunch friend, that we have enjoyed the best possible relations with a unified Canada. And I would leave it right there.

Future of Iraq

Q. Mr. President, I know you're following closely the reports from Iraq about the troubles that Saddam Hussein is facing. I'd like to ask you whether you think, if you feel he is near the completion of his regime? And are you concerned about some of the things that are happening there—I think now of the Iranian involvement. Are you concerned about possibly the Iranians having aggressive attitudes toward Iraq?

The President. Is that to both of us?

Q. Yes, sir. You first—whoever first.

The President. Yes, I'm concerned. I'm concerned about the instability. Neither the Canadians, nor the Americans, nor any other coalition partner wanted to see an unstable Iraq creating a vacuum in that part of the world. I'm not suggesting that is what is happening. But I'm concerned about it, and we are watching it with great interest.

What was the second part?

Q. I'm asking if Saddam is going to survive politically and are you particularly concerned about the Iranians? I mean, would you warn them not to try to take Iraqi territory?

The President. I think Iran knows our view; in various ways they know our view that grabbing territory would be counterproductive. And I could take this opportunity to suggest that that would be the worst thing they could do. And I know that I would speak confidently for our coalition partners in the Gulf on that point. I'd let the prime minister speak for himself.

On the question of Saddam, I have said over and over again that I think it's almost impossible—put it this way—is impossible to have normalized relations with Iraq while Saddam Hussein is in there. As the brutalities in Kuwait come out, as people see this environmental terrorism—right, looking it in the face over there—I think people are feeling more strongly than ever that what he has done in brutalizing that country and in the burnt, the scorched-earth policy, as he's violated every tenet of any concern for the environment, is beneath even contempt.

So, it is hard to see how an Iraq with him at the helm can rejoin the family of peace-loving nations. And, of course, there is this UN sanction question of damages that has to be addressed. But as one assesses the damage in Kuwait, I think the blame has to be put right squarely on his shoulders.

The Prime Minister. You can't find, I wouldn't think, a person in a civilized country who would do anything but expect and hope for a change in the leadership, a quite vile leadership that we have seen in Iraq.

To go to the first part of your question, one thing that Mr. Clark has picked up in the last week is an opinion quite contrary to the view that the coalition or the United States might adopt quite a leisurely pace in dealing with problems in the Middle East. There's a sense of urgency that Canada has picked up and we have conveyed to our partners about not sitting idly by and saying, well, perhaps six months or nine months or a year from now we'll get around to this. There is a request from all of the moderate Arab leaders who have been partners of ours in the coalition for prompt attention to some of the very serious matters that have emerged in the region.

The President. I'm a little nervous about my answer on Iran. I have no evidence that that's what Iran is trying to do. But as Iran has stated over and over again, their concerns about the US keeping some permanent foothold in that part of the world—I will say today that Iran must not and should not try to annex any of the territory of Iraq.

Having said that, being fair to the Iranians, I have no evidence, and I don't think the Canadians do, that Iran intends to do that. And I want to be clear on that point.

Jordan–US Relations

Q. Mr. President, there were published reports this morning that you had received a letter from King Hussein a couple of weeks ago, and that that letter has yet to be answered. Do you intend to answer it? And also, I'd like to ask if Mr. Clark's visit to Jordan was helpful in setting a new course for US relations with—

The President. Of course I'll answer his letter. I've expressed myself on the Jordanian question, on our relationship with the King, over and over again. But yes, I have received a letter, and yes, I will respond to it in normal course of events. I mean, it's not being held up; there's no delay, anything of that nature.

The Prime Minister. One of the reasons I asked Mr. Clark in particular to visit Jordan immediately after the hostilities was because King Hussein is, in certain quarters, below the salt these days. And Canada believes that he continues to play—notwithstanding his position in the hostilities, which we don't share, obviously—he continues to play and will play an important role in the future.

And we have made major contributions to the refugee problems that he has encountered. We have made other financial contributions because— and Mr. Clark had a very productive series of meetings with him—because we believe that, at an appropriate time, members of the coalition will of course want to resume a dialog with King Hussein. And we did not want that bridge to be permanently ruptured.

Mr. Clark, I can tell you, spent some hours with the King and his officials. And clearly, there's a desire on his part to resume progressively normal relationships both with the United States and the Arab leadership of the coalition.

Allied Consultations on the Middle East

Q. Mr. President, what specifically are you seeking in these allied consultations? Do you have some kind of idea of a coalition concerted action?

The President. On the consultations that Secretary Baker is having?

Q. And what you're doing here with Canada, France, and Britain.

The President. Well, a lot of our consultation today will be talking as coalition partners, long time friends, countries that are friendly, as to what we do about the Middle East. But we also are into some bilateral questions. And we are, after all, the biggest trading partner—Canada is our biggest trading partner, so we'll be discussing some trade questions as well.

But what I said earlier was not just boilerplate. We have seen eye-to-eye on the threat in the Middle East. And I am confident that when we talk to Minister Clark, who's coming back tonight, that I will get through his eyes and through the consultation with Prime Minister Mulroney a needed extra dimension on what's happening in that part of the world he's been. He's been into Syria; he's been to Jordan, I understand it; he's been to Israel. And of course, that question of Lebanon, the question of Israel, the Palestine question is all key.

We've got the Lebanon, we've got the Israeli-Palestinian question, and then we have the Gulf question. So, it is very important that coalition partners and normal friends as we are, stay in very close touch. So, that's what the consultation will be about.

Middle East Peace Process

Q. You mentioned the unity of the coalition in times of war. To what extent are you seeking unity in this postwar period, specifically on the Israeli-Palestinian question and the idea of land for peace?

The President. I've already expressed myself in terms of our continued support for [United Nations Security Council Resolutions] 242 and 338 that address themselves to that question. So, we are not backing off from that. But I think that we have a real opportunity. I think we have renewed credibility in that part of the world. I think there is a recognition in Israel that, in reducing the threat to them by the victory over Saddam Hussein, we've done something solid for peace. And I know there's that same sense of appreciation and understanding in the Gulf.

So, I think the coalition partners, such as Canada and the United States, are in the best position we've been in, in a long, long time not only to stay in touch and consult, but to get something done in these three areas that have been denied peace for far too long.

Cease-Fire in Iraq

Q. What is your assessment, please, of where we stand on the achievement of a permanent cease-fire and how it might affect the ability of US troops to be pulled out of southern Iraq?

The President. One, I'll restate my view that I want our troops to come home as soon as possible. I've just been elated as I've watched the troops come home and the warmth of the welcome and all of that. There are some details to be worked out on the cease-fire—the return of all the prisoners, accounting for those who have not been accounted for. I must confess to some concern about the use of Iraqi helicopters in violation of what our understanding was. And that's one that has got to be resolved before we're going to have any permanence to any cease-fire. And so there are several details remaining out there.

Q. Generally, are you satisfied with the progress, or do you think the Iraqis could do better?

The President. Very much satisfied with the progress that has been made since General Schwarzkopf met in the tent, but there are still some very important things to be taken care of, including the fact that these helicopters should not be used for combat purposes inside Iraq.

Palestine Liberation Organization

Q. Do you and the president see eye-to-eye on the role of the PLO under the current leadership?

The Prime Minister. My own opinion is the one that I gave the House of Commons the other day. I think that the credibility of the leadership of the PLO is zero. When you have people encouraging Scud missiles as they rain down on Israel and actively siding with the enemy in a major war, then of course you have people, as far as I'm concerned, of very questionable credibility.

Canada has always taken the position that there has to be a solution to the legitimate aspirations of the Palestinians. And it is up to the Palestinian people to choose their representatives. And it's not up to Canada or the United States or, I assume, anyone else to impose choices on them. But if we had our druthers, I think you can conclude what it might be.

For the life of me, I can't figure out why anyone would be supportive of a group of people who have displayed such consistently egregious judgement. But the United States may have a different view on it.

The President. I've expressed my disappointment in the PLO. The PLO, you remember—I believe it was at the Rabat summit years ago, was designated as the sole spokesman for the Palestinian people. But their leader chose wrong on this; went far beyond where he had to go in order to express his understanding about the dilemma that Iraq was in. Put it this way: he supported Saddam overly zealously and diminished his credibility—not any further in the United States, necessarily, because it had gone way down when those terrorist vessels came along the coast of Israel. But he diminished his credibility in the Arab world. He diminished his credibility with the coalition partners.

So, whether there is something that can come out of that organization that has been designated the spokesman for the Palestinian people that will be more reasonable or more sensible, let's hope there will be. But I don't think we're very far apart, if at all, on this with that the Canadian prime minister has said.

Arms Sales to the Middle East

Q. Mr. President, since you cited the reduced threat to Israel here this afternoon and your desire to halt the proliferation of arms in the region, are you reconsidering any potential arms sales to Israel, and is the administration reconsidering its pledge, promise, commitment—whatever you want to call it—to sell some billion [dollars] worth of arms to Saudi Arabia?

The President. When the Secretary of State gets back, we will be talking about that whole question. I have repeated my desire to try to curb proliferation. That doesn't mean we're going to refuse to sell anything to everybody. We're not going to cut off all weapons sales. We don't want to see imbalances develop. We won't want to see the threats to individual countries increased because of imbalance. But it is a subject, Jim [Miklaszewski, NBC News], that we will be talking about and trying to find an answer to.

I don't know what the questions are before the Congress now or the administration in detail on Israel requests. We think we've been pretty generous and fair in terms of this recent appropriation bill with the State of Israel. But I'll be reserving on that before going further until I talk to the Secretary when he gets back.

I would like to think that the diminished threat to Israel—and it is significantly diminished because of what's happened in Iraq—will be a reason that we will just not have ever-increasing arms sales.

You've got other countries, though, that want arms. The Saudi sale—that was put on kind of a hold, and I just can't tell you where that stands right this minute.

The Prime Minister. No one can fail to be struck by the irony of the fact that most of the hardware deployed in the Middle East was sold to the various factions by the five permanent members of the UN Security Council. This doesn't make a whole lot of sense if, on the one hand, you're trying to prevent war; on the other hand, there is the propagation of war through policies in the past that have led to this kind of development.

That's why Canada believes very strongly in the policies that we have put forward in regard to the control and possibly the elimination of these instruments of mass destruction. And that's why the president is examining this, because I think there is a general view, without getting into any question of a total interdiction for the moment that clearly a lot of these weapons—to understate the case—fell into hands that should never have had them in the first place. So, that is why our policy is predicated on that kind of activity affecting all of us.

Canada adheres to that policy today. I mean, we could be much more active in that area if we wanted. We have all the technology in the world. We have all the resources we need. We could be big arms merchants. We've chosen not to be, even though it's a very lucrative business. We've chosen not to be because it's fundamentally inconsistent with our policy—to develop it, to peddle it, to finance it, and then to deplore its use. And that is where Canada has taken a very vigorous and, we think, appropriate stand.

I know that in his comments earlier some weeks ago, President Bush alluded to the same problem and wants to rein in and circumscribe that problem. That's why we're where we are on this issue.

Canadian Unity

Q. And if I may, Mr. President, follow up on the previous question. You said that the United States enjoyed the best possible relations with a unified Canada. Does your administration have any concerns that whatever happened north of the border, trade or security arrangements with the United States could be jeopardized one way or the other?

The President. As I mentioned to you—maybe you missed that part of it where I said I didn't want to get into the internal affairs of Canada, courageously on the sidelines. But I will simply say that I'm not going to go any further than that, but I would put a lot of emphasis in what I said about how we value the relations with a unified Canada. I'm not going to buy into all kinds of hypotheses as what might happen.

But we are very happy—put it this way—we are very, very happy with one unified Canada that has been friendly, been allies—staunch allies. And when you have the unknown, you've got to ask yourself questions. But I'm not going to go into that any further.

The Prime Minister. Let me just answer the first part of the question. I've indicated to the president, as he knows, that Canada has gone through these constitutional difficulties in the past. We never minimize them because they're always serious. They're the product of our—we are the children of our environment. And families are and so are nations. But Canada's accomplished an extraordinary amount in 123 years. And I am satisfied that we will again over the next 123 years, although I'm not sure I'll be around.

The final question.

Soviet Union

Q. Could you tell me on the eve of the secretary's trip to Moscow whether you think it's your intention for your administration now to reach out in the Soviet Union individually to the Republics? And do you think that President Gorbachev's days are now numbered in power?

The President. I will continue to deal with the president of the Soviet Union. That is the government that's accredited, and that is the government with which the United States government will deal. We have had many, many contacts with leaders of the Republics including Mr. Yeltsin, including the Baltic leaders, including others that have been in the United States recently, including some that are considered opposition like the mayor of Leningrad. And we will continue to have those. But the last thing we want to do is to act like we are trying to determine the course for the Soviet Union in its internal affairs. So I will continue to deal—what was the last part?

Q. Whether President Gorbachev's days in power might be numbered.

The President. I think that everyone knows that he has extraordinarily complicated problems facing him. But, again, I think it would be imprudent for me to speculate on how he's going to master these problems. And so, I just would leave it there…

Trade With Mexico

Q. Thank you very much. Mr. President, I want to know if you envision a programme similar to this one with the Government of Mexico.

The President. You mean on the environment or on the trade?

Q. In both—trade. For the prime minister, I would like to know what he thinks of the trade agreement.

The President. On the trade agreement we are going to push very hard to get what we call fast track authority with the Congress. It is in the interest of the United States of America; it is in our own interest to go forward, say nothing about the interest of Mexico.

In Mexico you have a courageous new president who's taken that country and gotten relations with the United States in the best shape they've ever been in. And in terms of this trade agreement Prime Minister Mulroney, President Salinas, and I all agree that this trilateral approach makes a great deal of sense for all three of our countries. So, it is a priority, and we will push for it.

We have no environmental agreements of this nature that I can think of—I'll have to ask Mr. Reilly—that are in the works here. But I can tell you that we are working very cooperatively, more cooperatively than ever—and again, I salute President Salinas—with Mexico on environmental questions. We're doing much, much better in that regard.

The Prime Minister. Perhaps a word on the proposed trilateral agreement which would make North America the largest and richest trading bloc in the world, substantially more so than Europe. But I find we have already entered into a bilateral free-trade agreement with the United States. And we know it's productive, and we know it's going to be progressively so over the years. And that's because liberalized trade throws off new wealth. What I am astonished by from time to time are the protectionists whom I can understand but who, for example, in looking at Mexico—which is a developing country, and Mexico can achieve new prosperity either by aid or through trade. And trade ought to be the preferred route. If you're going to lift people up to a new dimension of prosperity then you have to liberalize trading opportunities for that country.

And the advantages work both ways. That is why President Bush's statement was so visionary: because while Canada and the United States had economies of equivalent degrees of maturity and compatibility, that of Mexico is in some areas less so. And it is an important step towards the integration of a developing country into a vast developed economy. And that is not only good for business, it's good for democracy because it gives individuals an opportunity to prosper through the ennobling means of trade, rather than through the instruments of aid and assistance which are a lot less noble than the opportunities that we can develop together. And that's why I hope that the trilateral measure that the president has outlined will get approval from the United States Senate and House and go ahead.

The President. May I add one point to that—just an observation. Not only has the United States got better relations with Mexico than ever, but Canada has demonstrated a keen interest always—historic—in this hemisphere. Recently joined the OAS. Been of a special help to many countries in the Caribbean area and also in Central and South America.

It is very important that while we focus on the Middle East and while we have our attention riveted on the changes of Eastern Europe that we not lose sight of the importance of this hemisphere. And I know the prime minister feels that way. And one of the things I forgot to mention… is the discussion, consultation of that kind of situation. We must not neglect it. And for the United States' part, we are trying not to—with our Enterprise for the Americas Initiative, for the Brady plan, for the work we've been doing in the Caribbean—and Canada extraordinarily supportive and side by side with us. So, we've got to move forward on the Uruguay round for GATT that's in everybody's interest. But we also must not neglect trade relationships in this hemisphere. And we're not going to, and I don't think Canada will.

The Prime Minister. Mr. President, I'm sorry, a final—this gentleman here has been trying.

The President. He's persistent.

France and the Palestine Liberation Organization

Q. Are you going to ask France—for both of you—not to back PLO as the official interlocutor of the Palestinian people?

The President. I have no interest in asking them not to back the PLO. I will share with President Mitterrand my disappointment over the way Yasser Arafat and some of his colleagues have behaved. And I will be probing with him to see if we can find a way to be more active catalysts for peace.

And let me say I'm looking forward to seeing President Mitterrand—because Mr. Mulroney and I were talking about this. We both have great respect for his knowledge of the Middle East. And we may have some differences with France. And, if so, I expect I'll hear them loud and clear down in Martinique tomorrow for lunch. But we also have a lot in common. And the common way we're looking at the Middle East these days far, far exceed the other. So, I wouldn't expect to find—and I'm anxious to ask him—that President Mitterrand was elated about the performance of Yasser Arafat, because France stood with this coalition early on—lots of pressures at times mounting at home—and solid as a rock also. And President Mitterrand led the way. Let there be no mistake about that one.

So, I think in your question, I'll be listening—"François, what are you going to say about this?"—because he knows a lot about it. But I know he'll be disappointed in the way the PLO reacted—acted as they drew the wrong side. Boy, did they choose it wrong. And now, we got to wait—a little time. But I want to see what he thinks about it.

News Conference at Skydome
Toronto
9 July 1991

The Prime Minister. I'm delighted to welcome the president and his party to Canada. We've had an opportunity for a very good review of the situation before the baseball game, in particular, the situation as it relates to the G-7 summit, upcoming in London next week. I think that the American and the Canadian positions are, in many areas, very compatible.

We—as far as Canada is concerned—we don't expect either blank cheques or miracles in London, but we expect President Gorbachev to arrive with a very serious plan to fundamentally reform the economy of the Soviet Union. And if that takes place, my expectation is that there will be a positive and constructive response from the members of the G-7.

I believe that's, by and large, the position of most of the leaders with whom I've chatted so far, and the president can tell you about his own expectations. But we had the chance to touch on this, the situation in Iraq, some bilateral matters where we have a very good bilateral relationship.

And so, I thank the president for his visit, and I look forward to the ball game a little later on.

Mr. President.

The President. I have nothing to add to what the prime minister said about the expectations for the G-7 meeting. But I will say this: that once again, I have found in the prime minister a man whose judgement I value on these matters. I think on Canada–US, the relationship is very, very good—the bilateral relationship. And as we had this *tour d'horizon*, we discovered that we were looking eye-to-eye at most, if not all, of these international matters.

So, it's a pleasure to be here. It's a night for baseball, but I, too, will be glad to respond to several questions.

South Africa

The Prime Minister. The question, Mr. President, was in regard to your response on sanctions, on South Africa. I indicated that Canada was part of the Commonwealth on sanctions, that we were going to stick to the sanctions until our common-front partners felt that we had met all the criteria, but in the case of the United States, you are guided by criteria from Congress and that you would be responding to that in your time.

The President. Well, let me simply add to that that, yes, the American law is clear. And when the conditions set out by Congress are met, the president will lift the sanctions. It's not a question of exercising a lot of judgement; it's a question of determining whether these five conditions have been met. And we are getting very close to making a final decision and I will make it in accordance with US law.

It is different than the Commonwealth arrangements that Prime Minister Mulroney referred to.

Q. Mr. President, I understand your interpretation of the law, but what do you say to the argument that black South Africans really won't be free of apartheid until there's a new constitution and they get the right to vote? And why not keep that pressure of sanctions on until South Africa goes over the top, so to speak?

The President. My view is, when the five conditions have been met, that it will be better for all South Africans to keep the process of reform moving forward. I think it will benefit their economy, and I think that will mean more jobs for blacks. I've never been enthusiastic about sanctions in the first place, if you want to know the truth. But I think that de Klerk has done things that none of us would have dreamed possible in effecting and moving towards change and freedom, and moving towards the ultimate, total elimination of apartheid.

And our law is clear. And I plan to not seek some way out of it, but I plan to enforce it. And I'll do it very cheerfully because that is my view.

Q. Are you confident that South Africa will go that final step?

The President. I'm confident that as long as we don't slap President de Klerk in the face after he achieves what we set out as goals and we do what we should do, I think that will encourage further development and further fairness and further elimination of racial barriers that are offensive to everybody.

Q. Apart from the different criteria that you've outlined in each country for the lifting of sanctions, would you say, in President Bush's words, that you see eye-to-eye on this matter as you do on other international matters? And is the sanctions question, whether sanctions should be lifted by Commonwealth nations, in any way linked to your own plans to visit that country in the fall?

The Prime Minister. No. We've had a disagreement with the American administration going back to the days when the president was the vice president. Canada firmly believed that sanctions were the only way to go in terms of bringing a racist regime to its knees, and bringing about the necessary changes, which is why we were in the forefront of the design and the application of the sanctions package in 1984–85.

Now, we always recognized that the American administration could quite properly take another course of action, which it did. We have implemented our sanctions, pursuant to a series of criteria which once met, we will change. We don't believe they have been met, and until we meet with the Commonwealth foreign ministers in the near future, we won't make that decision. But we recognize there's another school of thought in regard; there's no difference on the objective being sought. The objective being sought by President Bush and myself was always the elimination of apartheid. And there was no question about that. It was just the way of getting there.

But I think that we both recognize that President de Klerk has made some remarkable strides forward, and that has to be recognized and acknowledged and, indeed, applauded.

The President. It's very interesting—if I might, with your permission, sir—it's very interesting that in the United States, some of those senators who were in the forefront of putting into effect the sanctions laws are now saying it would be a mistake to continue the sanctions, provided these five conditions are met. For example, one of the most respected US senators is Senator (Richard) Lugar of Indiana, and I believe he is—and I know he was, early on, a strong advocate. But he also was in the forefront on the enactment—or the creating of these laws that govern what the president does, and he, I think, has said as recently as today that it would be appropriate if these sanctions are lifted in accordance with the law.

And so, I look at it, hey, I'm there to execute—they made the laws, and I'm there to faithfully execute and fulfill my obligations as president of the law.

Q. Today the IOC [International Olympic Committee] made a decision to allow South African athletes into the '92 Olympics. I'm wondering if this is going to change Canada's policy on not allowing Canadian athletes to participate in the same event as South African athletes.

The Prime Minister. There will be no change in our policy whatsoever. We devised our policies in conjunction with our fellow members of the Commonwealth some five or six years ago. We have executed them in tandem with all the members of the Commonwealth but one. And there will be no change in our policy until we have an opportunity to get together with our colleagues in the Commonwealth in the late summer.

Q. Does this mean that Canadian athletes then will not be sponsored to go to the Olympics?

The Prime Minister. Well, it means exactly what I said. There will be a meeting in the late summer or early autumn, and we'll try and deal with the matter then.

Soviet Union

Q. Mr. President, will Mr. (Aleksandr) Bessmertnykh (USSR Foreign Minister) and the rest of the team that President Gorbachev is sending to Washington find any willingness to give on the American position? And secondly, if these START talks are wrapped up this weekend, will that affect our posture, the G-7 posture towards aid to the Soviets?

The President. No, I don't think anything that's decided regarding START will have any effect on the thinking of the United States or these other countries. I think, as the prime minister very eloquently stated, we are in very close agreement as to what should happen. We are going to welcome Mr. Gorbachev there. I think it's a very good thing he's coming. But I wouldn't think that if there's a START agreement, that that would change for other countries this formulation, broad formulation we're talking about.

Now, in terms of the summit, I want to have a summit with President Gorbachev. I think it's a good thing. I did talk to my dear friend, Brian Mulroney, today about subjects that all of us need to talk to the Soviets about. You can't do it in one hour at lunch in London or with 18,000 observers in a multifaceted meeting in London. There are a lot of things we need to talk about.

But one of the criteria for having a summit has been, on both sides, a solution to the START question, as you know. And so, what we're going to do is to sit down with (Mikhail) Moiseyev (USSR's Chief of the General Staff) and Bessmertnykh, who have come in response to an appeal I made to President Gorbachev—and I thank him for that—to see if we can't iron out a couple of major technical problems with START and then a few other smaller problems.

But I don't want to overstate my anticipation on this because I'm not that sure we can hammer it out before I see Mr. Gorbachev for our bilateral meeting in London at all. I think that the very fact they are here is responding to one thing that I felt strongly about—is that we need to make clear to the Soviets that we are activating our bureaucracy in every way possible. And I think this is a very good sign on his part that he is willing. Secretary Cheney had plans that we were enthusiastic about, getting the poor guy a day or two of rest. He's turned around to come back to Washington. And we have demonstrated in every way we can how important we think these talks are.

But I don't want to raise the hopes of a lot of people in the United States and in other countries that want to see a START agreement. We'll wait and see. I don't know what's going to happen in these talks. But I think we've given and given, and I hope the Soviets understand that. And we've got to get in a deal that not only are we enthusiastic about, but one that can get through the Congress. So, I'll leave it right there.

Q. They won't find any more give in our position?

The President. I'm just not saying. When you go into a card game you don't—into a negotiating session you don't say, hey, by the way, we want to compromise on points a, b, d, or e. I mean, we'll sit down and talk to them. And we have given, and we have taken, I hope, a little bit, gotten a little bit of flexibility on their part. And that's the way this negotiation will be approached.

Q. The prime minister, in giving an account of your discussions on the future of President Gorbachev, referred to these changes of both political and economic survival. Do you, both of you, have any doubts of conscience about the changes of political or economic survival of Gorbachev?

The President. In the first place, I think that's a matter for the internal affairs of the Soviet Union to determine who's going to be in control there. I think when Mr. Yeltsin won that landslide victory and then came, at least speaking for the United States, came to the United States and spoke of new cooperation with Gorbachev, that was a good thing. I think—as I look at the situation, I think that is very much of a reassurance, if you will, that President Gorbachev will be around as president of the Soviet Union.

And so, we, for the United States, do not anticipate his demise in any way. And yet these matters, the final determination, obviously should be for the people of the Soviet Union to determine.

The Prime Minister. On that, when you have a country larger than the United States, with a population base larger than the United States, whose GNP is between 30 and 35, 40 per cent, perhaps, max, of that of the United States, you have a country in very serious trouble. Everybody knows that. Mr. Gorbachev happens to be president of that country whose system brought about the downfall of the economy.

He is coming to London, in our judgement, the judgement of Canada, as a man who has demonstrated great leadership instincts and great leadership examples. His reaching out to the United States and reciprocal responses have been very constructive and very helpful internationally. But he's got very serious problems that can only be addressed by fundamental reforms in his economy. And I suppose all we're saying in regard to the economic survival is that, indeed, unless there are strong moves towards a market economy within time frames, it's doubtful whether he can get it all done in a required period of time.

So, the response to him, I think, from all of us will be constructive and helpful. He has more than proven his worth as a very impressive leader. But on this, we're all from Missouri, and we've all got to be shown before—as I indicated elsewhere, we're not going to throw good money after bad. We want to help but we want to do it in a very constructive and appropriate way. And I think that's the general attitude of most of the G-7 leaders.

Chapter 4:

Interesting Bookends

1992–1993

Introduction

To this point, the editors have highlighted the successes of the Bush-Mulroney partnership in numerous areas of bilateral and international relations. As both leaders entered the last full year of their respective periods in office, however, domestic political triumph and success were not to be. A brief but damaging economic recession dimmed the chances for both leaders in the political arena. In the US, Bush was battered politically on all sides. An articulate, youthful and skilled campaigning Democrat from Arkansas named Bill Clinton was soon on the rise, while an eccentric independent, billionaire Ross Perot, also cut into Bush's numbers—creating a "perfect storm." And in November of 1992 when Americans went to the polls, Bush was, indeed, defeated.

In Canada, the recession—combined with the fallout from the Mulroney government's introduction of the GST consumption tax on almost all goods and services and the Bank of Canada's war on inflation which led to crippling interest rates for Canadians—brought the popularity of the Progressive Conservative government to historic lows. On the constitutional front, Mulroney's efforts to bring Quebec into the Canadian Constitution, "with honour and enthusiasm," as he had promised during his first election as party leader in 1984, were not to be. Though he three times received the unanimous consent of Canada's premiers in attempting to amend the Constitution—a historic feat in itself—Canadian voters defeated the Charlottetown Constitutional accord in a nation-wide referendum in October of 1992. From that point, Mulroney's days in office were numbered.

But in the midst of these political defeats for both men, their joint legacy was further cemented, regardless of the polls. In October of this final full year in office for both leaders, they were joined by Mexico's President Carlos Salinas in the signing of the North American Free Trade Agreement in San Antonio, Texas. The world's largest commercial market was thus born.

On his final weekend as president of the United States, George Bush brought his friend from Canada to Camp David to share with him his final hours at the historic presidential retreat that is nestled amongst Maryland's mountains and streams. The two men walked Camp David's trails together with their families as the clock wound down on the Bush Presidency. They reviewed their joint triumphs, discussed plans for the future and spent quiet time together with their wives as 20 January and the inauguration of Bill Clinton grew closer.

In that sense, Mulroney later reflected, "we're interesting bookends. The first trip that he [Bush as president] made was to Canada. He came up to our home there in Ottawa. And the last weekend that he was in office, four years later, Mila and I and the children spent it with [president and Mrs. Bush] at Camp David… those were the bookends of a tremendous relationship both professionally and personally."

On the afternoon of 20 January, former President Bush boarded the plane formerly known to him as Air Force One—whose call sign now belonged to his successor—for the flight home to Houston and to start a new chapter in his life. Just over a month later, Mulroney announced his own resignation plans and on 25 June, he too began the journey home to Quebec and into history.

James McGrath and Arthur Milnes

Remarks to the Forum of the Americas
President George H.W. Bush
Washington, D.C.
23 April 1992

I can't think, really, of a more important moment than now to convene again this Forum of the Americas. Over the last three years, we've seen our world literally transformed: the Berlin Wall torn down and Germany peacefully unified, the people of Eastern Europe and the Soviet Union liberated from communism, and South Africa's historic vote to reject apartheid. And we've seen Arab neighbours negotiating for the first time face-to-face with Israel, and a worldwide coalition under the banner of the United Nations stand up and turn back Iraqi aggression against Kuwait. And there's been a profound change with meaning for every man, woman, and child on the face of the Earth. And we have drastically reduced—and this is one I take great pleasure in having been a small part of—we have drastically reduced the threat of nuclear war.

And just today, the United States took steps to facilitate trade in high technology goods, an initiative made possible by the changed strategic environment and the peaceful rebirth of freedom in the formerly Communist lands. We relaxed trade restrictions on exports, that served us well during the cold war era, but are no longer necessary in our new world. And our actions today will eliminate requirements for thousands of export licenses, including many that affected computers, one of our strongest export earners. Trade covered today by today's deregulation amounts to about .5 billion.

Here in our own hemisphere, the Americas have launched an era of far-reaching and hopeful change. We've made history, all of us. We're well on our way to creating something mankind has never seen, a hemisphere wholly free and democratic, with prosperity flowing from open trade.

From Mexico City to Buenos Aires, that vision is becoming a reality. For the first time in many years, more private capital is flowing into the Americas for new investments than is flowing out. In country after country, the hyperinflation that literally devastated the region's economies, particularly its poor, has been halted. In nearly every nation, real growth has returned. A growing number of nations are taking advantage of the Brady plan, an important initiative of our administration designed to reduce the debt burden on our neighbours and set the stage for the renewal of growth. Barriers to trade and investment are coming down. Go to the financial centers of the world, and you'll get the same message: one of the most exciting regions for investment is Latin America.

Alongside this economic revolution, we have witnessed and played a vital role to shape a political revolution just as powerful. Two years after we initiated Operation Just Cause, Panama has replaced the repression of the Noriega era with freedom and democracy. In El Salvador, after 12 years of civil war, our consistent efforts have brought peace. In Nicaragua, we succeeded in our goal of restoring peace and democracy through free elections. And throughout Central America, civilian presidents hold office, and the principle of consent of the governed is now firmly established. And in South America, Chile and Paraguay have rejoined the community of democracies.

This peaceful revolution throughout the Americas did not happen by accident. It is the work of a new generation of courageous and committed democratic leaders with whom we have worked closely in pursuit of common goals, those leaders supported by this dynamic private sector that is so beautifully represented here tonight.

The new spirit was demonstrated in June of last year, when the OAS General Assembly passed a resolution designed to strengthen the international response to threats to democracy. Consolidating this revolution will not be easy; we understand that. Millions of people in our hemisphere are still mired in poverty and political alienation. Recent events in Haiti, Venezuela, and Peru remind us that democracy is still fragile and faces continued dangers. In all our nations, powerful special interests cling to old ideas and privileges, promote protectionism. They resist expanded trade.

For the diehards, for Castro's totalitarian regime, for those in the hemisphere who would turn the clock back to military dictatorship, for the stubborn holdouts for economic isolation, I want to make one point clear: hundreds of millions of Latin Americans share a faith in human freedom and opportunity. And I stand with them. And as long as I am president of this great country, the United States will devote its energies to the true and lasting liberation of the people of the Western Hemisphere.

Sharing the democratic spirit makes a difference on every issue we care about. Democracy's rebirth led Argentina and Brazil to join hands to halt the spread of nuclear arms. Democracy energized Brazil to slow deforestation of the Amazon rain forest. Democracy gave Argentina the will to stop the Condor ballistic missile programme financed by Libya and Iraq. Colombia's democracy is leading the fight against the drug trade and working to restore its economic vitality. The restored democracy in Panama has passed tough new laws to combat money laundering, and it's working to renew its importance as an East-West trade corridor.

Make no mistake: political and economic freedoms are linked; they are inseparable. And just as people have a God-given right to choose who will govern them, they also must be free to make their own economic choices.

When we lift barriers to economic freedom within and among our countries, we unleash powerful forces of growth and creativity.

Before I leave office I want manufacturers in Cleveland to enjoy virtually the same access to markets in Monterrey as they now have in Minneapolis. And with new technologies, creators of services in Denver may be able to tap markets in Santiago as readily as those in Chicago. I'll work to ensure that government protection and excessive regulation don't stand in their way. To do this, we'll have to overcome the stunted vision of some special interests. And I am determined that we can and will do exactly that.

I've made it a top priority to conclude a free trade agreement designed to remove all tariffs on trade between the United States, Canada, and Mexico. This agreement will build on our historic free trade agreement with Canada. The success of the agreement with Canada demonstrates how free trade can benefit all concerned.

We cannot achieve this breakthrough by equivocating between the status quo protectionists and the movement for freedom and change. Some suggest that we can hide in a cocoon of protection and pretend still to benefit from the fresh air of competition. Well, if there's ever an audience that understands this, you and I know that is simply wrong-headed. Our economic future must not depend on those who pay lip service to free trade but full service to powerful special interests. We cannot have it both ways.

In our own War for Independence, those who took this kind of stand were known as the "summer soldiers." And they wanted the glory of the revolution without showing the gumption to stand for freedom even in tough times. Our stand is clear; my stand is clear: open trade is vital to this country, to the United States, and every bit as vital as domestic reforms to renew our system of education, health care, government, and administration of justice.

A free trade area comprising the United States, Mexico, and Canada would be the largest market in the entire world: 360 million consumers. Mexico—and I salute its president, its business people here tonight— Mexico is among the fastest growing national markets for US exports today. And over the last three years alone, American merchandise exports to Mexico have increased by two-thirds. Our exports of autos, auto parts, telecommunications equipment to Mexico have doubled. And while members of this audience may be aware of this, I doubt it is widely known in the United States that two-thirds of all imports into Mexico come from the United States.

It's not just the border states that profit from this growth. During my presidency, 45 of our 50 states have increased their exports to Mexico. Our top ten exporters to Mexico today include Michigan, Illinois, New York, Louisiana, Pennsylvania, Florida, and Ohio, as well as Texas, California, and Arizona, those border states.

Trade with Mexico already supports hundreds of thousands of US jobs. And just as an example: thousands of good jobs in Warren, Ohio, and Rochester, New York, depend on sister plants in Mexico to keep their products competitive. A North American free trade agreement would create thousands more. It would create competitive efficiencies and economies of scale that will help American companies compete in world markets.

Free trade with Canada and Mexico will make all of us winners in economic endeavour, but our relationship goes well beyond trade. We share borders that span the continent. We're linked by centuries-old ties of family and culture. I share a warm friendship with Prime Minister Brian Mulroney of Canada, whom I consult frequently. I count President Carlos Salinas also as a dear friend. And he and I have been promoting the "spirit of Houston" ever since our summit meeting just after both of us were elected in 1988. And both President Salinas and Prime Minister Mulroney are bold and imaginative leaders, and I am committed to working with them to forge enduring friendship among our countries based on open trade, cooperation, and mutual respect.

Now, you may have heard some suggest that politics will dictate delaying the North American free trade agreement until after the election. Well, let me say this: these voices are not speaking for me. The time of opportunity is now. I have instructed our negotiators to accelerate their work. I believe we can conclude a sound, sensible deal before the election. I want to sign a good agreement as soon as it is ready. And there will be no delay because of American politics.

Now, to other friends here let me say this: the North American free trade agreement is only a beginning. Our Enterprise for the Americas Initiative already has made noteworthy progress to open markets, expand investment flows, reduce official debt, and strengthen the environment throughout the hemisphere.

The Enterprise for the Americas Initiative reflects a revolution in thinking. Through this initiative, the United States is not seeking to impose our ideas on our neighbours. Rather, our programme is designed to empower them to succeed with free market economic reforms they've chosen on their own, ideas developed in Latin America for Latin Americans.

The courageous Latin American leaders who are reforming their economies and breaking down barriers to trade and investment need our support. And they are the true liberators of our era. True success will mean opening up statist systems formerly rigged to protect wealthy elites and closed to working people and the poor. Free market reforms will banish burdensome regulations that now prevent the urban poor from starting new businesses or campesinos from gaining access to credit and title to their land. Economic reform must also include honest government. Corruption is the enemy of both growth and democracy. New investment will flow only where the rule of law is secure, the courts are fair, and bidding processes are open to all.

The United States' economic destiny is linked to Latin America's. No army of protectionists can change that. When Latin America suffered its debt crisis of the early eighties, 1980s, we suffered through a corresponding drop in trade. We did. If you don't believe me, ask Caterpillar workers from Illinois or employees from Cessna in Kansas. Ask them if they suffered when our best customers in Latin America were in crisis.

With the rise of democracy and economic reform, US exports to Latin America have surged by nearly one-third in just two years… This is a much faster rate of growth than for our exports to Asia or Europe. It points to the fact that a stable, prosperous Latin America is a natural market for United States goods and services. Strengthening our neighbours' economies will result in more exports and more good jobs for people in the United States.

When any of us speak with our friends outside the Western Hemisphere, we need to assure them as clearly as possible there is nothing exclusionary in our vision of open trade and economic integration in our hemisphere. Our aim is simply to lower barriers to economic freedom within and among the nations of the Western Hemisphere, not, I repeat, not to create any barriers between ourselves and the nations of Africa, Europe, and Asia. All of our aims are consistent with the global policies of GATT.

I want to assure you I urgently want to open up global markets through success with the Uruguay round. We all, all of us from whatever country in the Western Hemisphere, have a stake, a big stake, in a successful conclusion of the Uruguay round of the GATT.

And if the equivocators and the protectionists and the pleaders for the special interests want to debate this, bring them on. I will take the case for increased trade to the people in every corner of the United States of America. And I will make this abundantly clear: free trade means more exports, more investment, more choices, and more jobs for Americans. Our great country is the number one exporter in the world… And we will knock down barriers, wherever we find them, to open markets, for instance, for our computer software, movies, books, and pharmaceuticals. We will fight hard against protectionism both at home and abroad.

And five centuries ago, a man of courage and vision set sail from Europe searching for new trade routes and opportunities. And he defied the timid counsel of those who said the Earth was flat. Christopher Columbus's voyage to the Americas transformed human history. Columbus was an entrepreneur, and the risk he took 500 years ago continues to pay off abundantly today. And today, we still have to combat the flat-Earth mentality, the mind-set that urges us to barricade our borders against competition, to shut off the free exchange of food and machinery and skills and ideas.

But the future does not belong to the status quo. It is the legacy of people like yourselves, people with far-sighted vision and then a spirit of enterprise. The future awaiting the Americas is a time of rediscovery, a time for empowering the poor through new investment, trade, and growth, a time for cultural renewal. Our efforts and the efforts of millions of citizens of the Americas can achieve new gains for honest, democratic, limited government. And together, we can usher in a new order of peace, a new time of prosperity, both animated by personal freedom.

Thank you all very much for what you are doing to strengthen free trade in this hemisphere. And let me say again how grateful I am to David (Rockefeller) and the other leaders of this wonderful organization for vitalizing and getting that private sector involved in all of these decisions. It is an absolutely essential ingredient if we are going to succeed in a course that is mutually beneficial.

News Conference
The White House
20 May 1992

The President. I think we covered an awful lot of ground in a short time. And just a couple of observations: I know that many are focusing on our trade issues, in particular on trade disputes. Well, that's natural. We've got this enormous, this immense trade that goes on between our two countries... I believe that this trade is of enormous benefit to the two economies and demonstrates vividly the value of that Free Trade Agreement. And because of the large trade between the US and Canada, there are bound to be some bumps in the road.

We have existing mechanisms for dispute settlement. We are using them, including the FTA itself. And as a consequence, I can report that we're making progress in overcoming some of our recent problems. I told the prime minister, who forcefully presented Canada's case, that I would work with our administration to see that these disputes receive proper high-level consideration before they go to some form of action. I think this will help. But in any event, we discussed frankly the problems.

We also talked about a wide range of international issues, including the coming summit, including the G-7. So we had a very good conversation. And in the Bush view, our administration view, this relationship between Canada and the United States is very, very important to the people of the United States of America.

So, welcome back, sir.

The Prime Minister. Thank you, Mr. President.

As the president said, we had a very far-reaching discussion on a lot of subjects. I'd be happy to take whatever questions are appropriate.

But I tried to focus on what our priority problem is at this point in time, and it's trade. And for some time, Canadians have been troubled and angered by the attitude adopted by some people in Washington on major trade issues. Rather than move quickly to resolve or prevent irritants, the tendency was to retaliate against Canadian products by threatening to impose demonstrably unfair penalties on Canadian imports. These actions create uncertainty for investors and exporters and undermine the fundamental intent of the Free Trade Agreement.

The president has called me a number of times over the last few weeks, conscious of some of these difficulties that have arisen in a very complex and important trading relationship. We agreed at this meeting today to follow up on it. So we had a very constructive review of these issues.

We both intend to raise the level of commitment to resolve and to reduce disputes, to give a higher level of attention in order to manage the relationship and these issues. The president and I are going to work personally to that end. We both recognize that healthy trade between us is vital to recovery. We are the United States' best customer by far, and the United States is ours. We can help each other in terms of economic recovery by reducing the temperature and getting rid of a lot of these irritants, rather than allow them to fester and grow to important status.

For example, Canada's merchandise trade surplus was... the largest surplus since the second quarter of 1990, and for the first quarter, Canada's exports to the United States are up 8.8 per cent from last year. As the president has pointed out, even in a difficult recessionary period, the growth in trade between Canada and the United States is up very impressively. That means jobs in the United States and jobs in Canada, and we have to keep that going.

It was a very instructive and helpful meeting, and I thank the president and his advisors and counsellors and Cabinet ministers for that.

Canada–US Trade

Q. Who are these mysterious "some people?" Are you suggesting that the president himself may not know who in his administration, in your view, is discriminating against Canadian trade?

The Prime Minister. I've already indicated, and you know full well, that a lot of the action is initiated by industry, by interest groups, by lobbying interests in isolation from some of the fundamental objectives of the Free Trade Agreement. And in some cases, as dispute mechanisms have pointed out, they may or may not have validity. Sometimes the United States wins; sometimes we win.

What concerns me is not that. That's normal. What concerns me are demonstrably unfair matters being initiated and allowed to grow and fester when they should have been dismissed because the object of the Free Trade Agreement was to make it a model for the rest of the world or certainly a model for this hemisphere. And anything that vitiates, that undermines, the effectiveness of what is a very valid and helpful instrument for both of us. That's what I was talking about.

Q. Mr. President, do you agree that we have not been fair?

The President. I agree that when you have a trading situation that's as broad and as big as we have, there are bound to be some disputes. What we've agreed today is to be sure that we engage early on at proper levels to see that some of those disputes can be avoided. Some may not. Some may have to go to arbitration or to be adjudicated in legal manners. But I think we can do a better job of trying to avoid disputes. And that's what the spirit of these conversations were all about.

Q. Is the trade agreement jeopardized by this dispute?

The President. No. From our standpoint, we've got this agreement. I've cited for you the figures of advanced trade as taken place under the agreement. But what we've got to iron out are the differences, and they are overwhelmed by the common ground.

If you're referring to the NAFTA, I don't believe so. I think we just had a report on our side from our very able Ambassador, Carla Hills, who filled us in, and I detected no pessimism at all from her.

The Prime Minister. Helen [Helen Thomas, United Press International], from our point of view on that, we were very encouraged by the undertaking given today by the president to elevate the degree of attention that this trading relationship will receive in Washington by the administration. Oftentimes things get out of hand, but they tend to get less out of hand if the president is keeping an eye on it himself. That's what the president is going to work through his administration to make sure that they don't grow into the problems that they've become.

North American Free Trade Agreement

Q. Mr. President, will you be personally involved in the North American free trade agreement negotiations and talk to the prime minister about any barriers to completing those talks?

The President. Oh, sure. But I'm not going to be the negotiator. We've got a very able, experienced team that knows far more about the detail than I know, and they have my full confidence. But I have such a relationship with the president of Mexico and the prime minister of Canada that they feel free to call me on these matters, and I feel free to call them. If we are needed to finalize these agreements, clearly, all of us want to be involved, all three of us.

Canada–US Trade

Q. Prime Minister, do you feel you've received the kind of assurances that will allow you to tell Canadians they will no longer be subject to the kind of action you yourself described as harassment?

The Prime Minister. Well, we'll have to see. But I also mentioned at that time, as you'll remember, that I was satisfied that President Bush was a free trader and a fair trader. I've consistently mentioned that. I believe that the kinds of harassment that we've seen must stop. I think that the president understands that. He understands my concerns and has indicated that at the highest level he plans to work with Secretary Baker and Carla and Brent and others to make sure that this is conducted in such a way that it is brought to a halt, not to preclude valid cases from coming forward on both sides—.

Q. Sir, I was just wondering, based on your own experience, have you been able to give the president any personal advice on how to handle this plummet in the polls that he's experienced recently?

The Prime Minister. I remember a time when President Reagan was here. And there was a front-page story in the New York Times in August of 1987 that said, "President Reagan's popularity has just plummeted to 59 per cent." Right then I knew the difference between Canada and the United States: it's language. The word "plummet" does not mean the same in Canada as it does in the United States. So from where I'm sitting in the polls, I'm seeking advice, not giving any. [Laughter]

Canada–US Trade

Q. Any progress this morning on softwood lumber?

The Prime Minister. I indicated to the president that while we were encouraged by the reduction from 14.5 to 6.51, we still feel that this is a very unfair penalty on softwood exports from Canada that really do a lot of good for the United States. In fact, all that penalty is doing at the border is adding to the cost of an average house in the United States, which is why the governors in the Pacific Northwest are opposed to it. So what we're going to do is take this, under the Free Trade Agreement, under chapter 19, for resolution under the dispute settlement mechanism. I believe that Canada has a strong case and hopefully will win.

Q. Prime Minister, behind the trade dispute, is there a fundamental problem that Americans don't understand Canadian sensitivities on the trade issues?

The Prime Minister. No, I don't think that. I think the answer is the one that the president and I have referred to, that what it needs is an upgrading within the administration. In regard to the care and concern of—look, this is the most important trading partnership. A lot of Americans think their best trading partner is Japan. Wrong. Others think it's Europe. Wrong again. It's Canada. And the beauty of the trading relationship with Canada, unlike many others that the United States has, is that… at the end of the year [it is] in rough balance. The Americans are not carrying a big deficit to speak of in their trade with Canada. This kind of very valuable relationship has to be nurtured and looked after and admired for what it is. Otherwise, it could go the wrong way.

So it has nothing to do with Canadian sensitivities. It has a lot to do with upgrading this on the American side so that the American administration and people understand the importance of them not only to us but to them, and to use this as a model for trading agreements elsewhere in the world. I think it could be mutually beneficial.

Q. Mr. President. Can you tell me if you believe that Canada has been harassed by decisions on trade cases brought by senior advisors, including the man who is now your deputy campaign manager?

The President. I believe that we ought to look at the whole picture. And I believe that that enormous trading relationship has been marred by a very few number of disputes. And I can understand it when people feel very strongly on a deal, whether it's lumber or whether it's autos or whatever else it is that's contentious. I'm inclined to look at the whole picture and see it relatively free of dispute.

But when there is a dispute, I can understand the passions being very high. We've got to try to avoid the disputes before they take place, and when they do take place, each side has every right to take it to adjudication.

So I'm not going to try to characterize it, but when the prime minister feels strongly about something like that and tells me of his strong feeling, clearly I want to do what I can, working with our bureaucracy, see that any feeling of harassment is eliminated. We'll work to eliminate these, get rid of the disputes before they happen. But then, if they have to happen because we have diverse interests, we'll try to peacefully and harmoniously settle them.

So that's the way—I can understand the passions on issues on both sides of the border. But I believe that we can, with this spirit that the prime minister has outlined here, minimize the chance for future disputes arising, and that's what I think is coming out of this meeting.

So when he presents me with strong feeling, the view of Canada on some very contentious issue, I don't take offence; I say, 'Hey, let's try to work it out.' And similarly, I expect that when we go forward with something we feel very strongly about, and there are recent cases there, the prime minister says, 'Well, let's see whether we can't resolve that.' Sometimes they have difficulties in Canada. They have provincial governments; they have a central government, and we try to be understanding of that.

So I don't want to be standing here next to a good friend of the United States of America and a good free trader in some contentious mode. The meeting, albeit Brian Mulroney presents his case very forcefully—but I would simply say the meeting, as far as I'm concerned, some of it is let's find ways to avoid the disputes before they get to the point where one side or another feels harassment.

Q. Was there any discussion, sir (Prime Minister Mulroney), of the argument being made by some US senators that softwood lumber shouldn't even be allowed to go to a panel because it's exempted under the original FTA ruling?

The Prime Minister. No, we didn't get into the details of it… beyond what the president and I have indicated. But given the fact that we think that 6.51 is still unacceptable, we're going to take it to a chapter 19. And as I say, on behalf of the softwood industry in Canada, we think we've got a strong case and a good case, and that's what the dispute settlement mechanism is for. And we think that we can carry it successfully.

The President's News Conference With Foreign Journalists
Old Executive Office Building
The White House
2 July 1992

Multilateral Trade Negotiations

Q. Mr. President, in the last summits in Houston and London, there were nice words and beautiful commitments on the GATT negotiations, but no results. Do you expect the same in Munich?

The President. Well, I don't think the Munich summit will be dominated by the GATT talks. In fact, I talked to Chancellor Kohl in the last couple of days, and it is neither his desire nor mine, nor the desire of any of the European leaders or indeed Brian Mulroney or indeed Prime Minister Miyazawa, to have that happen. I think it will be talked about, but it isn't going to be the major area of discussion. I am still not giving up on trying to get something done before then. But there's very little time left. And we are still in constant discussion with various European leaders about this.

I'd like to have seen it worked out before then. But definitely progress has been made in closing the gap since the last—I believe you put it in the time frame of the last G-7 meeting. And a lot of the differences have been narrowed. But we still have some big ones, differences, and agriculture, as you know, remains the major stumbling block. But we're not going to give up on it. If we don't get something, some major breakthrough today or tomorrow, we're just going to keep on going because it is in the interest of the whole world. And I'll tell you the major beneficiaries of this would be the Third World. Trade for them offers them far better opportunities than just aid. So, we'll keep pushing on it.

North American Free Trade Agreement

Q. Mr. President, will you be signing a North American free trade deal in San Diego in a couple of weeks, as reported today by the Journal of Commerce, with Prime Minister Mulroney and President Salinas? And can you comment on the negotiations?

The President. One, I don't know about what we'll be signing. That is not a scheduled event at this time. I'd love to think we can get the differences ironed out by then, but I don't want to set artificial timetables. We've had some differences with Mexico, but I'll tell you one thing: the negotiations have been serious. Again, I'll give the same answer I gave on the Uruguay round, the differences have been narrowed considerably. They know the areas that we're having difficulties with, and we know theirs, but I just don't know about any timetable of that nature. It has not come to me that we are going to be ready. What has come from me to our negotiators is to get politics out of the way, if any is in there, and sign a good agreement so I can sign or initial a good agreement as soon as possible.

So I want to take this opportunity to say there isn't any politics involved in this. I keep reading, "Well, the President may not want to take a deal up to the Hill or have it on the Hill," and that is not true. It is in the interest of the United States of America to get a good free trade agreement with North America, with Canada and Mexico. So that's all. So we have no timetable set, but again it's like GATT. I'd like to just keep pushing and get it done as soon as possible. I talked to President Salinas about ten days ago and then subsequently talked to our negotiators. He's done the same thing. Jaime Serra, I believe, has been here. I know others have. And we're just going to keep on working on it.

Canada–US Trade

Q. Mr. President, did you give the steel case that was recently filed by the industry the top-level attention you promised Prime Minister Mulroney when it came to Canada, before the case was filed? And as a follow up, did you agree with the industry filing and including Canada?

The President. We give all these cases top-level consideration. We have laws in this country where people are allowed to bring their case to the various agencies. But, yes, I think that Prime Minister Mulroney had the distinct feeling that American politics were causing us to pull back into some kind of a protectionist mood vis-à-vis Canada. And I see enough of these cases to be able to say to myself that this is not the case. And when there's unfairness, the proper procedures will be followed. But I won't go into any specific case, but I owe him that kind of reassurance.

Yugoslavia

Q. Mr. President, you said that you're not ruling anything in or out with regard to Yugoslavia. However, very senior people in your administration have made it clear that you do not intend to commit ground forces. You have many tens of thousands of troops in Europe. That is a very major crisis taking place in a new Europe. If the United States is not prepared to commit ground forces in such a context, would it not be reasonable for Europeans to say, why are the Americans here, and for American taxpayers to be saying, what are we doing there?

The President. I don't know what spokesman you're talking about, but I've said nothing here about what I will or won't do. And under our system, the president of the United States makes those decisions on the commitment of forces or not to commit forces. That's one of the decisions that rests with me, not with anybody else, not the Congress, not anybody else.

So no decision has been taken on that. And I have had no pressure, to try to respond fully, from the United States Congress or any citizens here, to say why aren't we putting more troops into Sarajevo right now, for example.

I haven't had any feeling that there's a great demand for that. What we want to do is play our part in the fulfilment of the mission to bring humanitarian relief in there. But I don't think there's a great eagerness to put American troops there on the ground or to send NATO in there. The United Nations has a role; they're fulfilling the role.

So I think you raise a good point. But I don't think it will diminish support for NATO on the part of the American people. Or even from the Europeans, I don't think it'll diminish support.

NATO

Q. The question is, sir, if you're not going to intervene or not prepared or not very much inclined to intervene in a conflict of that nature even in theory, then what are you doing in Europe?

The President. We're there to guarantee the peace. And we're there to say, we know history. And if we'd have stayed there in the past with some presence, maybe we could have averted some of the disaster that befell Europe. We're there because Europe wants us there, too. Not only do we want to be there in a presence in the most efficient organization of its kind, NATO, but I think the Europeans all want us there. In fact, I keep asking to be darned sure I'm right on that question. And they do.

And so NATO is there. But that doesn't mean when you have a humanitarian problem here or you have internal divisions in any countries, and there are many turmoils based on ancient ethnic rivalries and hatreds that are cropping up, that automatically NATO goes to general quarters. That's not NATO's mission. There's ways to decide whether NATO should be involved or not. And I tried to recite the history here of the United Nations role. And in this instance the United Nations has taken the lead. Some individual European leaders have taken the lead.

But I don't see it as diminishing NATO's standing or certainly as diminishing NATO's commitment, the American people's wanting NATO to still have a strong US presence. Because the fact that they're not in this crisis, you might turn to me after I finish answering that one and say, what about some of the other areas where there are trouble spots going on right now in what used to be the Soviet Union? There's a lot of trouble spots. And my answer would be to that question, that because NATO is there and it is the most efficient peacekeeping organization that exists, that doesn't mean that it's going to be injected into every single crisis area. So there's other mechanisms set up for this one, and it's a very complicated problem when I look at it.

Somebody asked me, how is it different from, say, Desert Storm or from the invasion of one country from another? And as these countries sort out these enormously complicated problems, I make the point that that is different. They're internal to a degree, and yet they're new countries. But I make a point that it is quite different than the overt invasion of one country by another. I'm sure some in Sarajevo might not agree with that, but I think the mission for NATO has to be looked at in terms of each crisis or each outbreak of hostilities. And in this one, we've had other organizations that are trying to solve the problem. And you've had other countries that have been, on their own, trying to solve the problem.

But I will do my level-best to see that this does not diminish NATO. I am absolutely convinced not only do we have a role there, but it's an insurance policy, if you will, against the kinds of conflagrations that we've seen in the past. And so it will stay strong. And there will be some bumps in the road, but NATO is going to be the major organization of its kind anywhere in the world, I think.

This is the last one, and then I really, according to Marlin, must be off. Twenty-three minutes, 47 seconds.

Yugoslavia

Q. Mr. President, but the impression is that United States are maybe too cautious, too uncertain on the Yugoslavia crisis; they don't exactly know what to do. Can you tell me if it's correct or wrong?

The President. Well, I don't think that it's that we don't know what to do. I can understand somebody saying, well, why doesn't the United States use its magnificent military power one way or another to end all this suffering? But it's not that we don't know what to do; it is that we were trying to work with others in the ways I've outlined here to try to bring about an environment in which we can bring relief to the area. So, that's the way I would answer the question. Did I get it?

Q. Yes.

The President. Yes, that's about it. I mean, the United States is not going to inject itself into every single crisis, no matter how heartrending, around the world. And where we try to work with the United Nations, for example, we have no apologies for that. There will be times when we have to take the lead, when we have to move forcefully, when we have a clear mission. I am not interested in seeing one single United States soldier pinned down in some kind of a guerrilla environment. We go in there, we're going to go in there and do what we said we're going to do and get out. And this environment is a little complicated so that I could certify to the American people that's what would happen.

Q. Sir, what have you told Prime Minister Mulroney about the Canadian troops? Have you sent any special message to him as the Canadian troops went to—

The President. I gave him an "atta boy." I saluted him for doing what they're doing with the United Nations.

Q. Have you offered UN air cover for the convoy or any further convoys?

The President. Well, we have not been asked to do that. But they're doing a wonderful job over there. And I think the Canadians who have stepped forward deserve a great vote of thanks from the entire world for what they're doing. And when you see those pictures on the television and you see those courageous people there, why, we salute them. But he has not asked for that.

Let me put it this way: Canadian forces get in trouble, they've got some friends right here, right here, strong friends that are grateful to them and who respect them and have stood at their side before, and we're not going to let a lot of Canadians get put into harm's way without support. Put it that way.

President Bush's Remarks
Initialling Ceremony for the
North American Free Trade Agreement (NAFTA)
San Antonio, Texas
7 October 1992

May I start off by saluting President Salinas and Prime Minister Mulroney, Secretary Serra, Minister Wilson: welcome to the city of San Antonio. I thank the other foreign dignitaries, governors, mayors, and members of our Congress and my cabinet, so many from the business community from all three countries that are here.

We've just been talking about this, and this meeting marks a turning point in the history of our three countries. Today the United States, Mexico, and Canada embark together on an extraordinary enterprise. We are creating the largest, richest, and most productive market in the entire world, a $6 trillion market of 360 million people that stretches 5,000 miles from Alaska and the Yukon to the Yucatan Peninsula.

NAFTA, the North American Free Trade Agreement, is an achievement of three strong and proud nations. This accord expresses our confidence in economic freedom and personal freedom, in our peoples' energy and enterprise.

The United States, Mexico and Canada have already seen the powerful and beneficial impact of freer trade and more open markets. Over the past five years, as President Salinas reduced trade barriers under his bold reform programme and as Prime Minister Mulroney and I implemented the United States–Canadian Free Trade Agreement, trade between our three countries has soared. In 1992 alone, that trade will reach an estimated $223 billion, up $58 billion just since 1987.

If anyone doubts the importance of trade for creating jobs, they should come to this great state, come to the Lone Star State. In 1991, Texas exports totalled $47 billion, just from this state. And of that amount, over $15 billion went to Mexico, almost two and a half times as much as five years ago. This export boom goes well beyond one state, well beyond Texas. Virtually every state has increased exports to Mexico in the past five years.

NAFTA means more exports, and more exports means more American jobs. Between 1987 and 1991, the increase in our exports to Mexico alone created over 300,000 new American jobs. These are high-wage jobs. In the case of merchandise exports, those jobs pay a worker a full 17 per cent more than the average wage.

Free trade is the way of the future. I've set a goal for America to become, by the early years of the next century, the world's first $10 trillion economy, and NAFTA is an important element in reaching that goal. With NAFTA, as more open markets stimulate growth, create new products at competitive prices for consumers, we'll create new jobs at good wages in all three countries.

NAFTA will do these things and remain consistent with our other international obligations, our GATT trade obligations. Let me be clear that I remain committed to the successful conclusion of the Uruguay round of trade negotiations this year.

But NAFTA's importance is not limited to trade. We've taken particular care that our workers will benefit and the environment will be protected. As a result of NAFTA, the US and Mexico are working more closely than we ever have to strengthen cooperation on such important labour issues as occupational health and safety standards, child labour, and labour-management relations.

Then, on the environment, an issue of critical concern for all three leaders here today, we have agreed on practical, effective steps to address urgent issues such as border pollution, as well as longer term problems, such as preventing countries from lowering environmental standards to attract foreign investment. I salute the two gentlemen standing next to me, Prime Minister Mulroney and President Salinas, for their commitment and their leadership to this environment that we all share. As proof of that commitment, the United States and Mexican governments have already developed a comprehensive, integrated plan to clean up air and water pollution and other hazardous waste along the Rio Grande River.

I know for some NAFTA will be controversial precisely because it opens the way to change. Some of NAFTA's critics will fight the future, throw obstacles in the way of this agreement, to mask a policy of protectionism. But history shows us that any nation that raises walls and turns inward is destined only for decline. We cannot make that choice for ourselves or for our children. We must set our course for the future, for free trade.

Mr. President and Mr. Prime Minister: This accord underscores the principle that democratic, market-oriented nations are natural partners in free trade. We owe it to our fellow citizens to bring this agreement into effect as soon as possible, and I pledge my support to that end.

Remarks by Prime Minister Brian Mulroney at the Initialling Ceremony for the North American Free Trade Agreement San Antonio, Texas 7 October 1992

What we are marking here today is a signal accomplishment of leadership, vision and commitment. President Salinas, it was your commitment to opening up and modernizing your country's economy and to harnessing its huge potential that first inspired this initiative. Without your courage and resolve, these negotiations would never have happened, and this agreement would never have been realized.

President Bush… well, I think you and I have been through some of this before. Without your persuasive leadership in the implementation of the Canada–United States Free Trade Agreement, almost four years ago now, we would have had no FTA today upon which to build. The Canada–US trading relationship, which now exceeds $200 billion a year, is the largest such agreement between two nations in history. Our Free Trade Agreement has made that vast and complex association more mutually-enriching, predictable and secure. And, Mr. President, without your compelling vision of the Americas as a hemisphere of prosperity, built on cooperation—an approach strongly supported in Congress by many in the leadership of both major parties—we would not be in San Antonio today for this historic event.

I am convinced that the agreement initialled here by Minister Wilson, Secretary Serra and Ambassador Hills, and their own remarkable personal efforts in this negotiation, represent a grand accomplishment for North America and one that, I am certain, will be a proud contribution to the global trading system.

The North American Free Trade Agreement provides us all with a pathway to prosperity. For Canada, this goes hand-in-hand with the decision of my government to join the Organization of American States and play a more active role in the affairs of this hemisphere. As Canadians, we are also North Americans, and proudly so. While geography and the forces of history have made us neighbours, this agreement will make us partners—partners in opportunity and partners in the economic success that flows from free and fair trade.

As you know, four years ago Canada was on the verge of entering into the Free Trade Agreement with the United States. It was one of the most controversial initiatives in Canadian history. But our experience with free trade has been, in a word, beneficial—even during difficult economic times, and even while acknowledging the problems that ensue from restructuring and modernization. Our merchandise trade with the US is up almost 11 per cent during the agreement's first three years. Despite sluggish economies worldwide, in July Canada recorded its highest-ever level of exports and imports. For the first time, Canadian exports to the US exceeded $10 billion in one month, and the US has been strengthening its productive relationship with Canadian consumers. And I am confident that each of our three countries will grow stronger and more prosperous as our trade increases with the implementation of the NAFTA.

In each of our countries, important events are taking place. These truly are challenging times. It is all the more important that our three countries get on with the job of implementing the NAFTA, with all that it means for the future well-being of our peoples.

As you know, from the beginning of negotiations in Toronto to meetings in Mexico and the finale in Washington, this was an intense, demanding process requiring an absolute commitment to success from the three governments. Let us now succeed as effectively in securing the ratification and implementation of the agreement, further to the legislative requirements in our respective jurisdictions.

We all know that, while this is a trade agreement, it is not only about trade, not just about prosperity. For the first time ever, we have included in a trade agreement provisions that recognize our responsibility for the air we breathe, the water we drink and the land and resources that can serve us well only if we treat them well in return. As governments, we must also ensure that our people have the skills and training required to take full advantage of the benefits of this agreement.

The NAFTA, and the wealth it generates, will help us not only to prosper from our common interests, but also to celebrate our common values, our different cultures and our unique strengths. It is this human dimension that can never be entirely captured in a legal text, but which is an important benefit flowing from the agreement. The unity and cohesiveness we have fostered within our own borders, and which we will each reinforce in the days ahead, gives us the confidence to build economic bridges across those borders, ensuring better lives and greater opportunity for our peoples. For Canada, this has special meaning. Whether we are helping the United Nations through peacekeeping initiatives and development assistance programmes around the world or negotiating beneficial trade and economic agreements with neighbours and friends closer to home, there can be no doubt that we do it better as a confident, united country.

What has made the NAFTA a reality should also be an inspiration for a successful conclusion to the multilateral trade talks. We are resolved to make that a reality as well. There is still plenty to be done to get this agreement up and running. But I do see this as a most significant day for each of us and for the great countries we have the privilege to represent Mexico, the United States and Canada. The spirit of compromise, vision and commitment that helped forge this agreement will serve us well in the broad and impressive partnership that now links our three nations and that we will pursue together for the well-being of the continent we share and the people we serve.

Remarks by President George H.W. Bush
Honouring the World Series Champion Toronto Blue Jays
Old Executive Office Building
The White House
16 December 1992

This is about as much fun as I've had since the election, I'll tell you. I am just delighted that the Toronto Blue Jays are here. Ambassador Burney was to be here; I don't know that he is. But he's a good man. He's represented Canada well. And that brings me to the subject at hand. Is Steve—I can't see—

there's Bobby. Hi, Steve. Bobby Brown is here, an old-time, long time friend, the American League president, and I appreciate your being here, and Steve Greenberg, who is the deputy commissioner of baseball and doing a superb job in that very tough office. And I want to salute Mike Reilly and Joe West, the umpires. Very little good is said in kind about the umpires, but I'm glad to stand up for them. They do a great job. And our Little League champs are here from Long Beach, California. And behind them, I'm told, the Babe Ruth champs, Babe Ruth League champions from across the Nation. So welcome to all of you.

I wish that Carla Hills were here. You might say, 'Why?' She is our Trade Representative. And I thought she understood that our free trade agreement with Canada did not mean that the United States would trade away the world's championship. [Laughter] And most of these guys are very loyal to Canada and the Blue Jays, but most of them are Americans. And so we salute them as championship baseball players. I really am pleased that you could come down this festive time of year, and I'm proud to honour a team whose greatness transcends nationality.

The Atlanta Braves—it's like the Dallas Cowboys used to be, America's team, you know—the Atlanta Braves are known as America's team. And beating them, the Blue Jays became a true world championship team.

You know, I'm not sure in the World Series if it's getting more exciting each year or if I'm just enjoying it more. But this year's match up was a heart-stopper that baseball fans I don't believe will ever forget. Think of it: four one-run ball games, three Toronto victories won in the final time at bat. The Braves and Blue Jays staged a fall classic that even Ripley wouldn't believe.

And your season and this series were punctuated by some great individual efforts: Joe Carter, the man who brought you all home with the RBIs; Mike Timlin and the relief pitching crew who came up with some tight pitching at the end of very close ball games; the MVP effort put in by catcher Pat Borders, who couldn't be with us this morning—you see, his wife is due any day now with their second child; and then pitcher Jack Morris, who is here for the second year in a row. He manages to come no matter what happens. [Laughter] He came here with the Twins last year, and if he comes next year, we're going to give him a guest room—[laughter]—or get Governor Clinton to.

But, anyway, it was Old Man River's 11th-inning double in game six that put this series in the record books. And that hit, by a 41-year-old veteran, showed that baseball isn't about country; it's about courage and stamina and grit. And after 21 years in the majors, Dave Winfield finally has the World Series ring.

Cito Gaston, his coaching staff, and the entire Blue Jays team showed that America's pastime is becoming the world's pastime. And for that, as a fan, I could not be happier. By winning Canada's first World Series, you all became national heroes as well as cultural ambassadors, and you did it with class. You did it with class all the way. And class, of course, has marked the entire Blue Jays history. In 16 years, you've gone from the doghouse to the penthouse. Millie likes that. [Laughter]

Your general manager, Pat Gillick, will tell you those first few seasons were not easy. But in five of the last six seasons, Toronto has either won the American League East or finished second. And your fans have taken notice of your hard work. When you built the world's first convertible stadium, Skydome, who would have expected major league attendance records in 1991 and in 1992? More than 4 million fans each year.

Now, it's no secret that in the series, I had to—it was kind of an international thing; please, don't you guys be sore—I kind of rooted for the Braves, you may remember. [Laughter] But I've also got—and I'm not holding it against you all that you beat up my kid's team, the Texas Rangers, like you did. [Laughter] About the All Star Game, they were doing pretty well, until they ran into you guys from time to time; down they went. But nevertheless, that's another subject.

But look, I do want to congratulate the Braves also. They had another great season. They fought hard, and they never gave up. But in the end you won it, and you won it fair and square. And both personally and on behalf of the United States, I salute you. As I told Cito from Air Force One the day after the series, America is proud of you.

And in a larger sense I want to salute all of baseball, a game that I've loved since my dad took me to my first game—I think it was in Yankee Stadium—many, many years ago. In that spirit let me recognize the future major leaguers that are here this morning: the world Little League champions, the All Stars from Long Beach, California—you guys stand up for one second. There they are. Welcome, and I'm glad you came all this way. No speeches out of you guys; I'll do that. [Laughter] Okay. Special congratulations to the Babe Ruth League champs from Lexington, Kentucky, in the 6-to-12 division—where are they? You guys stand up. Thank you. And then from Phoenix in the 13-to-15-year-old division, big guys—where are they? Well done. And then lastly from Vancouver, Washington, in the 16-to-18-year-old category, we have some of those—there they are.

I hope all of you recall this day and these world's champions from Toronto. I can't think of better role models to follow or better examples of character: Fight clean and fair, and do your best.

Joe McCarthy, the great Yankee manager—Bobby, did you play for Joe?—once said, 'Give a boy a bat and a ball, and he'll be a good citizen.'

And those words are as relevant today as when I was playing baseball some 40 years ago, hitting eighth, second cleanup we called it. [Laughter] And to the heroes of baseball, young and old, I congratulate you on behalf of our nation, and I extend to you a very warm welcome to the White House. You've all excelled in that great American pastime we follow to this day, and so congratulations.

At this very special time of year, may God bless each and every one of you. Thanks for coming to the White House.

And now Cito, as a closing thing, I wish you'd come over here. This is a rookie ball player who needs a job. [Laughter] And I'm going to give you this baseball card. Take a look at him. You need a good-fielding first baseman; I'm your man.

Remarks by President George Bush on Signing the North American Free Trade Agreement
Organization of American States Headquarters
Washington
17 December 1992

Let me say at the outset how very pleased I am to be here. May I thank you for permitting us to have this ceremony here and welcoming us. I'm delighted to be back here. I've been privileged as vice president and president over the past 12 years to be here on quite a few occasions, and I am so thrilled that this, the final one, is to sign the NAFTA agreement.

I want to salute so many people here today. I see so many members of our Cabinet that worked diligently on this agreement, whether it was Commerce under Bob Mosbacher; or Labour, Lynn Martin; or the Environmental Protection Agency under Bill Reilly; the Interior with Manuel Lujan. We're all represented here today. And the list should be inclusive, not exclusive, because this has been a massive team effort on the part of the Canadian Government, the Mexican Government, and certainly the US side as well. But I do want to single out Ambassador Jules Katz, who is the deputy to Carla Hills sitting over here, who worked tirelessly on this agreement, and then, of course, our special representative, the US Trade Representative, Carla Hills, herself, sitting in the middle, who made this a labour of love and put everything she had into it. We owe her a great vote of thanks from the US side.

Many others at the State Department, from Jim Baker on, were extraordinarily interested in this, kept the diplomacy alive and moving forward, and I salute them. Bernie Aronson is with us today. I'm delighted to see him here. He, too, has taken this on as a very special project. Arnold Kanter, our Acting Secretary, today Acting Secretary of State, is with us, and as I say, Bernie Aronson. And of course, I would be remiss if I singled out Americans if I didn't mention one who came in with me here, General Brent Scowcroft, who's done an awful lot to see that the White House was fully involved in these proceedings. So, there we are. And again I salute two more: the Mexican Ambassador to the United States, Gustavo Petricioli, who's over here, and of course, Derek Burney, over here.

I know we have many representatives from other nations here, and I don't want to bore you with how things work in this country, but we have tried since the beginning of these negotiations to keep the various Members of Congress, the key Members of Congress, fully engaged in this, having them understand the gives and the takes that go with any complicated negotiation. And I'm very pleased to see several of the key Members of Congress, Members of the United States Senate here today. So, that's the American side.

Let me just now get on with some comments about this agreement and about the common business that brings us all together, the affairs of this hemisphere. Throughout history, the destiny of nations has often been shaped by change and by chance and by the things—when I say chance, I'm talking about things that happen to them. And then there are those unique nations who shape their destinies by choice, by the things that they make happen.

Three such nations come together today, Mexico, Canada, and the United States. And by signing the North American Free Trade Agreement, we've committed ourselves to a better future for our children and for generations yet unborn. This agreement will remove barriers to trade and investment across the two largest undefended borders of the globe and link the United States in a permanent partnership of growth with our first and third largest trading partners.

The peace and friendship that we've long enjoyed as neighbours will now be strengthened by the explosion of growth and trade let loose by the combined energies of our 360 million citizens trading freely across our borders.

I want to pay a personal tribute to my partners in this endeavour, two rare and gifted leaders, two special and valued friends without whose courage and leadership and vision this day could not have possibly come about. And when the history of our era is written, it will be said that the citizens of all the Americas were truly fortunate that Mexico and Canada, two great nations, two proud people, were led by President Carlos Salinas and Prime Minister Brian Mulroney. For Mexico particularly, especially, the

NAFTA is a bold undertaking, made possible by President Salinas's brave reforms to reinvigorate, to invigorate the Mexican economy.

It's especially fitting that an American President sign this agreement in this great Hall of the Americas, the home of the Organization of American States. You see, the NAFTA represents the first giant step towards fulfilment of a dream that has long inspired us all, the dream of a hemisphere united by economic cooperation and free competition. Because of what we have begun here today, I believe the time will soon come when trade is free from Alaska to Argentina; when every citizen of the Americas has the opportunity to share in new growth and expanding prosperity...

Today, as a result, the hemisphere is growing again. For the first time in years, more capital is flowing into the Americas for new investment than is flowing out. Every major debtor nation, from Mexico to Argentina, has negotiated a successful agreement to reduce and restructure its commercial bank debt under the Brady plan.

Let me just offer a brief aside about the Brady plan if I might. I remember telling my good friend Nick Brady, our Secretary of the Treasury, "Okay, we'll call it the Brady plan, but if it's successful we're going to call it the Bush plan." [Laughter] And he reluctantly accepted that guidance.

I think history will show that the leadership of our distinguished Secretary of the Treasury did pay off and the plan has been highly successful. And by the way, the name will always be, appropriately, the Brady plan. And that's the way it's going to stay.

Now, under the Enterprise for the Americas, many nations, Jamaica, Bolivia, Chile, Colombia, El Salvador, Uruguay, have reduced or shortly will reduce their official debt with the United States. The Enterprise for the Americas Initiative is working. The initiative allows interest payments on official debt to be channelled into trust funds that protect the environment and support programmes for child survival.

To those in other regions struggling to reform statist economies, Latin America shines as a solid example of hope that hyperinflation can be tamed, growth can be revitalized, and new investment and trade can accelerate if developing nations stay the course through the difficult challenge of economic restructuring.

These profound economic changes are a tribute to a courageous group of democratic leaders in Latin America and the Caribbean. Their revolutionary vision has altered forever the face of the Americas. Their friendship and counsel have been enormously gratifying to me as President. But these profound changes, along with the NAFTA itself, reflect a broader and, I believe, a more fundamental change in relations between the United States and the nations of this hemisphere. For many decades, we've proclaimed ambitious goals for ourselves of a good neighbour policy, of an alliance for progress, of a partnership built on mutual respect and shared responsibility. And those goals now are rapidly becoming a reality.

My talks with the hemisphere's leaders in recent weeks show a strong consensus that relations between the United States and its neighbours have never in our history been better, and that this development is working to benefit all of our peoples. And I take great pride in the fact that, working with those leaders, we've been a part of all of that.

I believe that in the future, America's relations with Latin America and the Caribbean will grow even stronger. I was pleased to hear our new President-elect, Bill Clinton, affirm that same goal in his remarks recently, both to the Rio group and to the Caribbean Latin America Action Conference.

This century's epic struggle between totalitarianism and democracy is over. It's dead. Democracy has prevailed. And today, we see unfolding around the world a revolution of hope and courage, propelled by the aspiration of ordinary people for freedom and a better life.

The world will long remember the images of that struggle: a citizen of Berlin, you know, sitting atop of the wall, chipping away with his hammer and chisel; Boris Yeltsin and his followers waving the flag of free Russia and defying the tanks and coup plotters. And here in this hall, it is worth remembering that those images were preceded by a democratic revolution in Latin America. No people struggled for freedom against oppression more bravely than the people of this hemisphere.

And here too, in the Americas, we are constructing a hopeful model of the new post-cold-war world of which we dream. This is the first hemisphere and the OAS is the first regional organization in the world to take on through the Santiago Declaration the formal collective responsibility to defend democracy. And in this hemisphere, the weapons of mass destruction, strategic missiles, as well as nuclear, chemical, and biological weapons, have been rejected voluntarily. And in this hemisphere, we've created new models of multilateral cooperation and success in resolving the conflicts that have tormented Central America.

As recent proof of the progress we've made, just two days ago we celebrated—and I'm sure everyone did—celebrated the end of the war in El Salvador. In this hemisphere, we have forged a new partnership to defeat the global menace of narco-trafficking, and we must succeed in that effort. And still we're not satisfied. The birth of democracy has raised expectations throughout the Americas, and now democracy must deliver. The communications revolution has opened the eyes of this hemisphere's citizens to the wider world. We're no longer blind to limits on legitimate political participation, to official corruption, or to economic favouritism.

If democracy is to be consolidated, the gulfs that separate the few who are very rich from the many who are very poor, that divide civilian from military institutions, that split citizens of European heritage from indigenous peoples, these gulfs must be bridged, and economic reform must ensure upward mobility and new opportunities for a better life for all citizens of the Americas.

To fulfill its promise, democratic government must guarantee not only the right to regular elections but human rights and property rights, swift and impartial justice, and the rule of law. Democratic governments must deliver basic services. Their institutions must be strengthened and must be modernized. To defend democracy successfully, the OAS must strengthen the tools at its disposal, and I commend the new steps that you took this week to suspend non-democratic regimes. Together we must also create new means to end historic border disputes and to control the competition in conventional weaponry.

In all of this, I believe my country, the United States of America, bears a special responsibility. We face a moment of maximum opportunity but also, let's face it, continued risk. And we must remain engaged, for more than ever before our future, our future, is bound up with the future of the Americas.

This is the fastest growing region in the world for US products. And in the struggle to defend democracy our most cherished values are at stake. Travel to Miami or El Paso, Los Angeles or Chicago or New York, and listen to the language of our neighbourhoods. We are tied to the Americas not just by geography, not just by history, but by who we are as a people. And no one knows that more profoundly than this proud grandfather.

This year marks the 500th anniversary of a voyage of discovery to the New World. And let this also be a time of rediscovery for my country, the United States, of the importance of our own hemisphere. If we are equal to the challenges before us, we can build in the Americas the world's first completely democratic hemisphere. Just think about that. Think of the importance. Think of the significance. Think of the example for the rest of the world.

This hemisphere can be as well a zone of peace, where trade flows freely, prosperity is shared, the rule of law is respected, and the gifts of human knowledge are harnessed for all.

More than 150 years ago, Simon Bolivar, the Liberator, whose statue stands outside this hall, spoke about an America united in heart, subject to one law, and guided by the torch of liberty. My friends, here in this hemisphere we are on the way to realizing Simon Bolivar's dream. And today with the signing of the North American Free Trade Agreement, we take another giant step towards making the dream a reality.

Thank you all very much for coming. And now I have the high honour of signing this agreement. Thank you.

[At this point, the president signed the North American Free Trade Agreement.]

Good luck to all of you now and in the future. God bless you.

Prime Minister Mulroney Speaking Notes
NAFTA Signing
Ottawa
17 December 1992

On behalf of Canada, I have today signed the North American Free Trade Agreement. Presidents Bush and Salinas are also placing their names on this agreement, in their respective capitals, today. Together, our signatures affirm a shared commitment to a new and cooperative economic arrangement in North America. Our three countries intend to secure the ratification and implementation of the Agreement well in time for its entry into force on 1 January 1994. Early next year, our government will submit the necessary enabling legislation for the consideration of Parliament.

I am joined today by many prominent Canadians who have devoted their skills, experience and enthusiasm to this negotiation. Also sharing this occasion with me are senior members of the Canadian negotiating team whose untiring dedication, under the leadership of International Trade Minister Michael Wilson, I acknowledge with genuine appreciation for a job exceptionally well done. A special word of thanks is appropriate for our chief negotiator John Weekes. His talent, drive and knowledge of the immense complexities of this deal made a successful conclusion possible.

The NAFTA, by bolstering our economic prospects, can strengthen our capacity as Canadians to chart our own course, and to continue working for the generous and uniquely Canadian society we cherish. Building as it does upon both the GATT and the Free Trade Agreement, the North American Free Trade Agreement is a logical reinforcement of Canada's strategy as a trading nation.

As Canadians, with our relatively small population dispersed over a vast landmass, we have always been critically dependent on trade. And we have benefited greatly from its bounty. That is why the North American Free Trade Agreement is in our long term best interests.

The positive impact of the Free Trade Agreement we concluded with the United States is now obvious. Compared to 1988, before the FTA, Canada's exports of goods to the US are now $17 billion higher. Over the first 10 months of 1992, exports to the US are up 11.2 per cent over their level a year earlier. Our merchandise trade surplus with the US has increased and a chronic foreign net direct investment deficit has become a surplus. Foreign direct investment in Canada has increased by $17.8 billion. And we have learned this morning that Canada's merchandise exports to the US have been at or near record levels in every month so far this year, hitting an all-time monthly high of $11 billion in October. If the trend observed through the first 10 months of this year continues until January, Canada's merchandise trade balance with the US for 1992 could reach $17 billion, the highest level since 1987. This year's surplus will be up more than 22 per cent over 1991.

Canada is also forecast by the International Monetary Fund to have an increase in labour productivity over the 1992–1993 period of 5.2 per cent, compared to 2.4 per cent in the US. And, for the first half of 1992, our unit labour costs, relative to those of the United States, have fallen by more than five percent.

In a competitive world where only productivity increases can generate genuine new wealth, these indicators are especially heartening. We are also encouraged by the OECD report released yesterday that suggests that economic growth in Canada is projected to increase by 3.2 per cent in 1993 and 4.2 per cent in 1994—the highest growth rate among the G-7 countries. The OECD also states that Canada will lead the G-7 in terms of employment growth, with our inflation rate among the lowest of industrialized nations in the world. These are most impressive signs for countries like Canada, for whose citizens international trade constitutes their economic lifeblood.

Now, after the FTA, comes the North American Free Trade Agreement, which will create the world's largest free trade and investment area with a combined population of 360 million and a Gross Domestic Product of almost $8 trillion. The NAFTA offers the prospect of attractive rewards for successful Canadian businesses and their workers, and a potential springboard for breaking into additional Latin American and other foreign markets.

President-elect Clinton has indicated that ratifying the NAFTA will be one of his priorities. And later today, I will meet with British Prime Minister John Major and with the President of the Commission of the European Communities, Mr. Jacques Delors, to discuss the prospects for an ambitious global trade liberalization emerging from the GATT round of multilateral trade negotiations. I can confidently assure them that the North American Free Trade Agreement is consistent with the GATT obligations, indeed that the NAFTA complements and builds on the GATT principles to which Canada attaches such fundamental importance.

The challenge for Canadians is clear: either continue to recover our competitiveness relative to our trading partners, or forfeit our standard of living. By becoming more competitive within North America, Canadian companies will be able to take on global markets. Open markets and fair rules will reward these companies with increased opportunities abroad. And new trading opportunities abroad for our companies means more and better jobs for Canadians here at home.

That is the path we have chosen—not because it was the easiest or the most popular, but because it was the best and most direct path towards a better, more prosperous future for all Canadians. But we still have much to do together. Business and labour must join together with both federal and provincial governments. I am sure that Canadians will recognize that the North American Free Trade Agreement is a good agreement for Canada, a good deal for Canadians.

I commend Presidents Bush and Salinas for their foresight and leadership, and join them in celebrating the common opportunity that our respective nations now share.

News Conference of the President and the Prime Minister
Camp David, Maryland
16 January 1993

The President. May I just say how wonderful it is to have the prime minister of Canada here with us today, great friend of the United States. The relationship between Canada and the United States is strong; tremendous trading partner. Prime Minister Mulroney has done an awful lot in all ways in cooperating and working with us. Their leadership in many areas of peacekeeping is one that we respect and admire. He was the one that prodded me to do more on environmental legislation.

And so for me and for Barbara, this is a fond farewell as we leave this job. And it's most fitting, in our way of looking at things, that Prime Minister Mulroney and his wonderful family are with us here today. So we're going to talk some business, and then we're going to look around and have a little R&R.

The floor is yours, sir. Welcome.

The Prime Minister. Thank you, George.

Well, we're delighted to be here. The president has pointed out the strength of the Canadian-American relationship. It's, as you know, a huge and a complicated one and not always an easy one. But it indicates the extent to which neighbours can become friends and mutually assisting partners.

Canada is the largest trading partner that the United States has, and you are ours. And so President Bush's visionary initiative in respect to free trade throughout the hemisphere is one part of a very important legacy that he will be leaving.

The Clean Air Act that gave rise to the Canadian-American treaty on acid rain is another very important matter that people in both countries had fought for literally decades.

And I can tell you that, because I happened to be there, that his remarkable assembling of the coalition in terms of the Gulf war ... is probably without precedent, certainly in recent decades.

So I'm delighted to have a chance to come by and say hello to the president and the family before he leaves office. And of course, he'll always have the friendship and the respect of Canadians.

Iraq

Q. Are you with him now in this current standoff with Iraq?

The Prime Minister. Yes, I am.

Canada–US Trade

Q. Prime Minister, you said there would be structural changes in the relationship between Canada and the US to avoid some of the trade irritants when you were last here and met with the president. Do you think they'll survive the new administration, or will you have to work to put them in place again?

The Prime Minister. Well, I think we have to work hard at trade at all times. It's a difficult matter because it affects jobs sometimes in both countries, and so it's not easy. And we're going to have to work hard to maintain this relationship, as we did in the past. Fortunately, in the past we had a friend in the White House, and I suspect that will be the case in the future. Governor Clinton understands and has told the president—

The President. That's right.

The Prime Minister.—and told me of his recognition of the great importance of Canada as a trading partner and a friend to the United States.

The President. No question about that. No question about that.

Iraq

Q. Mr. President, what's your response to Aziz, Mr. President? Are there any more warnings?

The President. We have no response now. We're interested in knowing what the United Nations response is. It's the United Nations going on with this; it's the United Nations, Dr. Ekeus, that we'll be talking to. And we'll all be talking about that a little later. But his move just was announced, and we'll just have to wait and see how it's regarded. We don't do these things unilaterally. We consult. We'll be able to talk now with the prime minister. We'll be talking with others as well, I think, during the course of this afternoon.

Canadian Ambassador

Q. What signal did you hope to send to the Americans with the appointment of General de Chastelain? Was there a message in it in terms of the role and expanded relationship we want with the United States?

The Prime Minister. No. He's just an outstanding Canadian, a remarkably talented man who can do a very good job for Canada in Washington at a crucial moment. And he's held in very high regard. In fact, he'll be here this afternoon at Camp David.

The President. Yes, I'm looking forward to that.

Q.—push them on the UN or other matters?

The Prime Minister. Well, we're not pushing anybody. He'll be there to defend our interests.

Canada–US Relations

Q. President Bush, what is your assessment of Canada–US relations as you leave office? Have they improved?

The President. Thumbs up.

Q. Still any problems that have to be worked out?

The President. None. Well, once in a while you can run into a little hiccup, a little bump in the road. Once in a while we've had some differences on trading problems. But look, you've got to look at the big picture. And the relationship is outstanding. It's important. I mean, it is vitally important to the United States. It's important today, was yesterday, will be tomorrow. And so it really is fundamentally sound and good and strong.

Iraq

Q. Sir, have we moved back from the brink of military action that you hinted at yesterday?

The President. We're not on the brink or moved back from anything. We're just going to be consulting, and we'll see where we go from there. I wasn't trying to be belligerent. I'm just simply saying they're going to comply with these resolutions, period. And so we'll see.

Q. Well, was it more conciliatory, their response today? Was there any movement?

The President. Well, we're going to talk about it. I mean, I've learned something about this. You don't jump to conclusions until you know all the facts, get all the translation. I heard him. What I heard in English sounded—that he was going to let these people in, but we've got to wait and see. I don't know about these conditions and all of that. But those are the things you consult about. He's thrown some conditions on it.

Camp David

Q. How do you feel about leaving Camp David?

The President. Leaving Camp David? Well, I'm not leaving until—[laughter]—Monday night. But Monday night if you ask me, I expect I'd feel sad about that. This has been a wonderful retreat here, and I've sure enjoyed sharing it with friends, domestic and from overseas. And this weekend is going to be pure joy because we've got some good friends here.

Q. What have you got in store for the Prime Minister and his family?

The President. A lot of exercise. A lot of exercise. [Laughter]

Final letter from George Bush as sitting President
to Prime Minister Mulroney
17 January 1993

I think it is fitting that you were my last guest as my presidency is drawing to a close. As you recall, my first presidential trip was to Ottawa in February 1989. I remember the contrast between the bitter cold outside, and the warm friendship we kindled in our conversation that day. Through good times and bad, I have been comforted by the fact you have been a wise counsel, a strong supporter, and a true friend. Our efforts to ensure smooth implementation of the FTA and to bring the dream of NAFTA to reality should be the envy of all. I want you to know, however, that I have never seen relations between our two countries as only the sum of trade issues. I have never wavered in my belief that when Canada remains engaged in world affairs, then democracy, peace, and freedom are advanced. I think back to Desert Storm and how leaders like yourself committed your countries without reservation to ensuring that Saddam's aggression would not stand.

I think back to those perilous hours in 1991 when the future of the Soviet revolution hung in the balance. Your strong opposition to the coup gave hope to democratic forces in Russia and silenced critics who said we had not done enough to help then President Gorbachev. Your counsel in handling the transformation in the Soviet Union—from strengthening Yeltsin, to managing delicate relations between Ukraine and Russia—has been invaluable. Canadian soldiers keeping the peace in Latin America, Europe, Africa, and Asia are testimony to Canada's commitment to bring about a true and global collective security. I could go on and on—Bosnia, Haiti, the Middle East.

It's a record that should make every Canadian proud. It's a record that brings to life the true meaning of partnership between our two countries. Although my public life is coming to an end, Barbara and I will be cheering you on. Now, as always, our love to you, Mila, and the children.

P.S. Brian, You're a true friend. It will ever be thus as far as I'm concerned. Good luck.

President Bush with his Secretary of Commerce Robert A. Mosbacher, Sr.

Prime Minister Mulroney, President Bush and Prime Minister Margaret Thatcher of the United Kingdom share a light moment at an international summit. US Secretary of State James A. Baker III was part of the conversation as well.

A rare glimpse inside the Cabinet room in the Parliament Buildings in Ottawa as the Mulroney cabinet becomes the first since Prime Minister Louis St. Laurent's to send Canadian forces into combat. The picture below, which shows Ministers Barbara McDougall and Tom Hockin, reflects the tension in the air.

In 1991, after the end of hostilities in the Persian Gulf, President Bush again visited Ottawa for discussions with Prime Minister Mulroney.

The President and the Prime Minister are joined on Parliament Hill by Canada's Ambassador to the United States, Derek H. Burney and US National Security Advisor Gen. Brent Scowcroft.

The Prime Minister late at night in Japan on a secure telephone call with President Bush.

*The leaders and their wives, First Lady Barbara Bush and Mila Mulroney,
at Kennebunkport, Maine, 1991.*

Arguably the most significant accomplishments of the joint leadership of the President and Prime Minister: The Canada–US Acid Rain Accord being signed in March 1991 (above) and the signing of the North American Free Trade Agreement (NAFTA) in October of 1992 (below).

The 41st President at 24 Sussex Drive, The Official Residence of Canada's Prime Minister with Canada's Royal Canadian Mounted Police on hand in Red Serge.

Still close friends today. George H.W. Bush, Barbara Bush, Mila Mulroney and Brian Mulroney, Kennebunkport, Maine, 2008.

134

*January 1993, a walk in the woods at Camp David on the
final weekend of the Bush Presidency.*

Chapter 5:

A New Sense of Partnership

1993 to Present Day

Introduction

In political retirement, both George Bush and Brian Mulroney, along with their families, have maintained the close friendships established during their years in office. They still gather each year at Kennebunkport and love nothing better than an evening spent reviewing the international scene—with no need to feed the press with a photograph or quote.

In 1994, Mulroney participated in the dedication ceremonies of the Bush Library on the campus of Texas A&M University in College Station, Texas and remains active in the institution's affairs. Both men have taken part in academic symposia on both sides of the border examining the end of the Cold War, the 10th anniversary of the Canada–US Free Trade Agreement and NAFTA. Both have as well stated their cases before history in various books and interviews over the years.

This year, 2009, marks the 20th anniversary of the inauguration of Bush as the 41st president, an event that took place just two months after Mulroney became the first conservative Canadian prime minister to win back-to-back majority governments since Sir John A. Macdonald, Canada's first prime minister, in the 19th century. Still, 20 years is not long enough in the grand sweep of history to render a conclusive and objective verdict. There are signs, however, definite signs, that history will be kind to George Herbert Walker Bush and Martin Brian Mulroney.

A united Germany is now one of the powerhouses of Europe with a vibrant and strong democracy; and despite occasional flare-ups involving Russia, the Cold War is history and Europe remains at peace.

In both Canada and the United States once fierce opponents of the NAFTA are now amongst its greatest champions, and the new generation of leadership in both countries tinkers with the deal at their own political peril.

But above all else, both Bush and Mulroney have left in their joint wake a model for cooperation and leadership between Canada and the United States that remains an example to all nations and for American presidents and Canadian prime ministers who take office in the decades to come. Few would argue that their shared legacy of common achievement forms part of the foundation on which the future of North America will be built.

In Washington, DC—a town steeped in symbolism—it is noteworthy that the only embassy on Pennsylvania Avenue, the city's most prestigious address, is the Canadian mission. In fact, Prime Minister Mulroney officially opened the embassy in its new location in May of 1989 and he and then Vice President Bush had laid the cornerstone in 1987. Given their many contributions to this vastly important bilateral relationship, perhaps it is fitting, then, that this cornerstone of that diplomatic headquarters bears the names of these two leaders, two gentlemen, two partners, two friends.

James McGrath and Arthur Milnes

The Right Honourable Brian Mulroney
Bush Presidential Library Foundation Tribute
Houston, Texas
29 November 1994

No honour could give me more pride than being here tonight to pay homage to a great American President and a true friend, George Bush.

James Joyce once wrote that: "The past is consumed in the present and the present is alive only because it gives birth to the future." Nothing better illustrates the truth of those lines, which refer to the majestic cycle of human life and personal endeavour, than tonight's tribute to the public service of George Bush: the son of a United States senator who, as a young man, served as a navy flyer in the Pacific, congressman, director and ambassador; in later years, himself the president of the United States; and now, as he enjoys the golden years of a brilliant career, father of the governor-elect of Texas and the next governor of Florida.

As the decades unfold and the children and grandchildren of George and Barbara Bush make their own contributions to the public service of this nation, there will be few precedents in modern history to equal the accomplishments of this remarkable American family.

What we celebrate tonight—our admiration and affection for George and Barbara Bush—is actually the "sizzle," as delightful as that might be.

The "steak" is the contribution they both have made to America and the world.

I am especially pleased to be part of a group ensuring that the manifold dimensions of a genuinely impressive presidency will soon be captured at Texas A&M for generations of Americans to come. And what will they learn of the Bush presidency?

As prime minister of Canada for nine years, I worked as closely with George Bush as vice-president and president as any other leader in the world—perhaps even more so. I saw him privately, up close, when great decisions of peace and war were made. I saw him at crucial G-7 summits around the world, at NATO meetings in times of crisis—and around the swimming pool at Kennebunkport when our major problem was explaining to the media why the fish had avoided us for another day!

In the very brief time I have tonight I would like to give you a few impressions of the man and what I view as some of his most significant achievements.

President Truman used to say that "a page of history is worth of volume of logic." Let me tell you why I think history will rank the Bush presidency highly and why our grandchildren will speak of President Bush as a "visionary." The word is deliberately chosen—and, contrary to some earlier journalistic views—I believe fully justified.

Reinhold Niebuhr wrote with great insight:

Nothing worth doing is completed in our lifetime; therefore we must be saved by hope. Nothing fine or beautiful or good makes complete sense in any immediate context of history; therefore we must be saved by faith...

It is in this perspective that great and controversial questions of public policy must be considered.

Time is the ally of leaders who placed the defence of principle ahead of the pursuit of popularity. And history has little time for the marginal roles played by the carpers and complainers and less for their opinions. History tends to focus on the builders, the deciders, the leaders, because they are the men and women whose contributions have shaped the destiny of their nations.

Theodore Roosevelt had courageous leaders like George Bush in mind when he spoke at *La Sorbonne* and said:

It is not the critic who counts; not the man who points out how the strong man stumbles, or where the doer of deeds could have done better ...The credit belongs to the man who is actually in the arena, whose face is marred by dust and sweat and blood... who spends himself in a worthy cause, who, at the best, knows in the end the triumphs of high achievement and who, at the worst, if he fails, at least fails while daring greatly, so that his place shall never be with those cold and timid souls who know neither victory nor defeat.

And so, let me outline briefly some of the powerful issues resolved during the presidency of George Bush.

1. In the second year of the Bush presidency, the Soviet Union imploded. This was the most epochal political event of the 20th century. No single occurrence and no single individual was solely responsible.

    But the names of Ronald Reagan and George Bush will be prominent and proud when history casts in concrete the definitive version of the major events of the era.

    The Khrushchev goal of "burying" the West was demolished and, in the dramatic 70 year confrontation with the Soviet Union, the cause of freedom had overwhelmingly triumphed. This extraordinary victory was achieved and the explosive aftermath safely secured in very large measure by the military strength and strategic foreign policy direction of the United States of America, led skilfully by President George Bush. And he did much of it personally—in meetings or by telephone—not through emissaries or messages drafted by committees.

    An ominous situation that could have become extremely menacing to world security was deftly channelled into the building of an embryonic democracy in a country that had been ruled by czars and tyrants for a thousand years.

2. As the Berlin Wall collapsed and calls for freedom cascaded across Central and Eastern Europe, leaving dictators and dogma in the trash can of history, no challenge assumed greater importance and acuity for Western solidarity than the unification of Germany within a strong European Community and an unswerving NATO. But old fears in Western Europe and implacable hostility in the USSR rendered this initiative among the most complex and sensitive ever undertaken. One serious misstep and the entire process could have been compromised, perhaps irretrievably.

    I remember the two plus four meetings in Canada, the tense and difficult negotiations with President Gorbachev, the frequent conversations in Ottawa with Ambassador Ed Ney and meetings in Washington and around the world with President Bush, Vice President Quayle, Jim Baker, Dick Cheney and Brent Scowcroft.

    There is obviously no more knowledgeable or competent judge of what really happened at this most vital juncture of 20th century history than Chancellor Helmut Kohl of Germany himself. In a speech to a parliamentary commission last year he said categorically that this historic initiative of German unification could never have succeeded without the leadership of President George Bush.

3. Much has been written about the Gulf War. Simply put, the coalition of 29 disparate nations assembled under the aegis of the United Nations and led by the United States will rank with the most brilliant and successful international initiatives ever undertaken in modern history, designed to punish an aggressor, defend the cause of freedom and ensure order in a region that had seen too much of the opposite for far too long.

When President Bush was beginning to focus on the magnitude and complexity of this crisis in the immediate wake of the invasion, he invited me to the White House for a private evening of highly confidential discussions. At the end of what turned out to be a lengthy and serious debate and review of all factors, he set out for me his views on keeping NATO solidarity intact; defined the potential umbrella role that the United Nations Security Council had to play; discussed how our personal relations with moderate Arab leaders could be used to ensure their indispensable participation in repelling Saddam Hussein; and forecast a battle wherein we would prevail—and here I am quoting him directly—"if we strike swiftly and overwhelmingly from the air."

That conversation took place a full six months before the war began. I have always been struck by such an uncommon display of prescience and assurance by a world leader confronting one of the greatest threats to international security since the Korean War.

4. The completely improbable image of a peace treaty being signed on the White House lawn by Prime Minister Rabin of Israel and Chairman Arafat of the PLO is a direct consequence of allied success in the Gulf War. Any objective historian will be able to draw a straight line from the new geopolitical realties that emerged in the Middle East from the end of the Cold War, to the immediate aftermath of the Gulf War to the Madrid Peace Conference, to the Oslo discussions, to that ceremony on the South lawn of the White House.

I was in full agreement with the decision of the Committee to award Prime Minister Rabin, Foreign Minister Peres and Chairman Arafat the Nobel Peace Prize for this magnificent achievement. History will know, however, that the names of President Bush and Secretary Baker deserve to be inscribed on the same award.

5. In October 1992 I joined Presidents Salinas and Bush in San Antonio, Texas, to sign the NAFTA—the North American Free Trade Agreement among our three nations, creating the largest and richest free trade area in the world—360 million people generating seven trillion dollars of goods and services annually... Thomas Macaulay wrote in another century: "Free trade, one of the greatest blessings a government can confer on a people, is in almost every country unpopular." It initially was in Canada and in the United States, although both nations strongly embrace free trade today.

    Carla Hills, Bob Mosbacher and others in this room carried the US brief in this arduous initiative.

    The decision to proceed was made by President George Bush in his nation's interests. Without him, there would not have been a NAFTA—it's just as simple as that.

    And the truth is that, in terms of job creation in the United States, no single action by an American president since the Second World War will produce greater long-term benefits for the American economy and those of this hemisphere than the decision to proceed with NAFTA—in spite of powerful, strident and politically damaging opposition.

6. And finally, President Bush's decision, strongly supported by Administrator Bill Reilley, to go forward with strong environmental legislation, including the *Clean Air Act* that resulted in an Acid Rain Accord with Canada, is a gift to future generations of Americans to savour in the air they breathe, the water they drink and the forests and streams they cherish.

In these six major illustrations I have chosen, there are a number of common threads: Most of these initiatives were very controversial, bitterly opposed, and with the prospect of few immediate political benefits. But all of them were ultimately successful and all of them will bring long-term strengths to the United States and to the world. They were an integral part of George Bush's vision of the world and America's role in it.

There is a word for this: it is called "leadership"—and let me tell you that when George Bush was president of the United States of America, every single head of government in the world knew they were dealing with a genuine leader—one who was distinguished, resolute and brave.

Robert Samuelson recently noted that: "Some people mistake salesmanship for leadership. There are times when people should be told what they need to know and not what they want to hear." Well, that is what George Bush did and that is why I believe historians will view much of what he accomplished as visionary. They will say, decades from now, that he had the courage to take decisions not for easy headlines in ten days but for a better America in ten years.

And as the poet, Robert Browning, wrote:

Ah, but a man's reach should exceed his grasp
Or what's a heaven for?

Skeptics and the uninformed think, and sometimes say, that nations only have interests. That selfish definition of citizenship is greatly misleading because nations, like people, are neighbours and can become genuine friends. Indeed, over 50 years ago, Churchill described the relationship between Canada and the United States as: "An example to every country and a pattern for the future of the world."

It was in this way that Mila and I became friends with George and Barbara Bush. They are truly exceptional human beings—warm and generous, faithful and fair—with whom we have shared challenges and accomplishments that were at once glorious and delightful and sometimes sentimental and sad. But through it all they conducted themselves at home and around the world in a manner that always brought honour to the United States of America.

Free Trade @ 10 Conference
Montreal, Quebec
From Canada to Mexico:
"A Common Future"
George H.W. Bush
June 1999

I'm pleased to be here to celebrate the legacy of an agreement that represented the best of international diplomacy. And I say this because whether you're talking about the FTA, the Free Trade Agreement, between the US and Canada, or NAFTA between Mexico, Canada and the US, each agreement reflected a mutual commitment by the respective countries to build a common future based on shared values, rather than always dwelling [...] on past differences.

I was pleased to see this conference not only looking back at what happened, how NAFTA came to be, but also looking forward to the future, to the challenges that clearly remain. My presidential library, of which I am so proud, at Texas A&M University in College Station, has hosted some conferences. And my dear friend and colleague, Brian Mulroney, was kind enough to participate in one of them, as we had a look at the events that led to the end of the Cold War and to challenges that lay ahead. The George Bush School of Government and Public Service at A&M also had a great exchange with Canadian and Mexican students on NAFTA, and I loved being a small part of that.

The point is that conferences like this one offer a great opportunity to look back and forward and, if you'll kindly indulge me in a personal observation, I'm so pleased that several members of my team participated and will participate in this conference: James Baker, Carla Hills, Clayton Yeutter, Peter McPherson, and of course, Bill Reilly, our environmental expert. I don't believe any American president was better served by the men and women who stood at his side, and I believe Brian Mulroney and Carlos Salinas were equally well served by their team-mates. I am very pleased that Jaime Serra, who was instrumental, a key instrument in negotiating the NAFTA agreement, is here today.

One thing is sure: we came together to work at a dramatic time in history. We had a rare opportunity to build a new partnership with our hemispheric neighbours as the day the dictator was yielding to a new dawn of democracy and market capitalism. We wanted to help foster this trend. As vice-president, I supported the Free Trade Agreement with Canada, and as president I was committed to continuing opening markets for American goods, services and farm products. We recognized that exports were a growing element of economic growth, so we naturally had an interest in finding better access to more markets.

We sought to expand free trade through a number of avenues, the Uruguay Round at GATT, bilateral negotiations with Japan, active involvement in the development of APEC, and our Enterprise for the Americas initiative, the Brady plan—these were but a few of the things we tried to do.

Without a doubt, NAFTA became a critical cornerstone in our trade strategy. It doesn't seem possible, but just nine years ago this month Carlos Salinas and I presented the product of our negotiation, which Canada had been advising on all along, and that Canada promptly joined. And having come into office about the same time, the Mexican president and I had been able to forge a new spirit of cooperation. For my part, I thought it was absolutely essential to my country that we have close relations with Mexico as we had long enjoyed with Canada, and expanding free trade through the NAFTA, lowering the trade barriers between our people, was part of that effort.

In dealing with him on NAFTA and a host of other issues comprising the US-Mexico bilateral relationship, President Salinas's word was always good. A trained economist, and a committed free trader, I think our work together had real merit. And I'm sorry that he has these difficulties, but I think we would be remiss if we did not pay tribute to him for his key role in the NAFTA agreement.

As for Brian Mulroney, with whom I first worked with as vice-president, after I became president, and as our relationship became closer, my respect for him only grew. I always appreciated his wise counsel, his constructive criticism—he could be very frank with the criticism, believe me—and he'd offer these things up. We'd talk very frankly about US–Canada issues, and also on issues of global import. I learned a lot from your prime minister. And perhaps that was indicative of how similarly we saw some of the fundamental issues we faced as leaders of our respective countries.

It was also a reflection of the fact that far more often than not, I think the people of Canada and the US shared similar values. In any event, while I expect Brian paid a political price for being perceived at times to be too close to us, maybe to me, I can tell you, however close our working relationship was, that Prime Minister Mulroney always had Canada's interest at the forefront of whatever discussion, never yielding on principle as to what was best for his country.

NAFTA was but one good example. After we were both out of office, Brian confided that during the debate over NAFTA, at one point his political support was down to the members of his immediate family, and he was a little suspicious of Mila, as a matter of fact. I know the feeling: I'm an expert on how polls can be high one day, and down the next. Like Brian, I felt the benefits of NAFTA far outweighed the downside for workers and companies, that it would create far more winners than losers. Moreover, speaking from my perspective, it was in the interest of the US to see Mexico and Canada grow their economies, to say nothing of our own, in ways that created widespread prosperity and thus further enhancing regional stability.

And yet, as clear as the reasons were for fighting for NAFTA, given the increasingly partisan mood prevailing on Capitol Hill, I knew that NAFTA would be a tough sell, and I wasn't disappointed. Leading congressional Democrats, including the top leaders of that party in the House of Representatives, backed by labour, and joined by some in our party, on the "right wing" you might say, fought us tooth and nail all the way. It was a passion-filled debate. At times the rhetorical barrage coming from the opposition both on Capitol Hill and around the country got a little out of hand. One prominent American, I prefer to keep him nameless, went so far as to predict there would be a "giant sucking sound"—you know who I mean.

There's been no giant sucking sound. You've heard the statistics, those of you attending this conference, but here's just a couple of them. Since NAFTA took effect in 1994, over 16 million jobs were added to the payrolls in North America. That's 16 million new citizens with the hope of building a better future. On a parochial note, US–Mexico trade has doubled, growing at 17 per cent annually; and in the process, Mexico surpassed Japan as our second-largest trading partner.

Meanwhile, US trade with Canada, already our number one trading partner, continues to grow at 10 per cent annually. Also, NAFTA is widely credited with helping to stabilize Mexico following the peso devaluation, in the aftermath of that crisis.

Meanwhile, more recently in the US as the Asian currency problem resulted in a significant drop in our exports to Asia, growth in our trade through NAFTA has protected jobs. Indeed, with US unemployment at its lowest rate in decades, it is simply not credible for anyone to say that NAFTA is costing us in terms of net jobs.

True, the US lost some manufacturing positions last year, a figure that was used was 385,000, but at the same time we gained three million new jobs in advanced sectors such as computer programming, management consulting, and all kinds of services. Everywhere you look at in North America, it seems that the job market is being transformed, and the trends for the most part are in the right direction.

Now, does this mean our work is done? Far from it. And yet regrettably the momentum that so many people worked so hard to build towards getting NAFTA passed has not been sustained. I can't speak for Canada, but I can talk about the United States in this regard. With the Cold War behind us, many countries are still struggling to develop and adopt policies to negotiate the geopolitical landscape still in a state of flux.

In my country, some people are using uncertainty and ambiguity of the moment to create a momentum for turning America selfishly inward, away from the world. Even though they deny it, they advocate policies that amount to protectionism and isolationism. Their slogans "Come home America," and "America First."

This is selfish; this is beneath the history of my great country, but it's out there, and it worries me, this coalition of left and right. I just simply think that these views are wrong. On trade, that same odd coalition that fought me earlier this decade, the far left joined by the far right, remains intact, and no doubt these elements were emboldened by our inability, President Clinton's inability, to secure the so-called fast-track authority. This power is necessary so the president can negotiate a clean treaty without mindless amendments being placed on it.

The treaty then goes to the Congress and has to be voted up or down. Without that fast-track authority, it is impossible for any president to negotiate a trade agreement. I believe that loss of fast track sent a horrible signal to the world not simply in this hemisphere, but I know it sent a bad signal to Asia and to Europe as to what the heartbeat, as to what the intent of the United States is. They wonder if we are backing away from our commitment to free and fair trade.

Meanwhile, the world is not waiting for us to muster renewed resolve as Canada has shown by securing further free trade agreements with Chile and Israel and others. Suffice to say I hope the United States can find a way to move forward with Chile, and engage the member states of MERCUSOR. As I stated as president, I hope to see the day that our hemisphere is totally united under free trade agreements for the Americas, and I might add that as soon as Mr. Castro leaves the scene, I hope—I know—our hemisphere will be united in democracy.

With regards to global trade, I hope that we can continue to find ways to eliminate, in a responsible, forward-looking way, barriers to trade. I might say parenthetically that I hope China soon becomes a member of the World Trade Organization. It makes no sense at all to keep China on the outside looking in.

I hope that agreements like NAFTA will lead to the elimination of trading blocs that pit one region against another. I believe the NAFTA and the FTA were not just steps to expanding free trade north and south, but also east and west. I hope that we'll hold up our end of our agreement, and make sure NAFTA is fully implemented by 2008. The complexity of the issues that remain to be ironed out are a testament to the difficulties we've faced in securing the peace; and yet at the end of the day, in spite of all the new challenges that remain, I am more optimistic about the future than at any time in my life. I believe that my grandchildren have the opportunity now to live in a very, very peaceful and productive, harmonious millennium.

I think we all have to work towards that end. As we near the end of this decade, and look at the challenges and opportunities, much work remains to secure the full promise of peace, justice and growth. Looking around this room at this distinguished gathering, and last night having the opportunity to interact with some of Canada's leading businessmen and academics, I believe we all seek the same thing. But to reach our goals, it is absolutely imperative that our respective countries continue to work to maintain the kind of partnership that at its core recognizes and values international cooperation as the key component to building the brighter future we all seek.

Brian Mulroney did that. Others in Mexico, the United States, and in Canada must step forward now and emulate his commitment to free and fair trade. Sometimes you have to take the political heat to get something majestic done for your country and, indeed, for the hemisphere. It's called leadership; and we need more of it.

Free Trade @ 10 Conference
Montreal, Quebec
The New Economic Environment
Brian Mulroney
June 1999

As you know, we are rarely able to evaluate within a few years the real impact of important decisions of public policy. Most often, it takes a great deal of time, even decades, before all the consequences of an important initiative are apparent.

In the recent history of our country, there have been several major policy decisions whose impact is still not completely known. One such initiative was the Canada–US Free Trade Agreement. Few events in the short history of our country have aroused such passions and controversy. The debates were often bitter and indignant, and it took a general election to convince Canadians to ratify the FTA.

The adversaries of free trade didn't mince their words. It meant the end of our social programmes, of health care, of regional development programmes and of our cultural identity. Even our sovereignty was threatened.

The proponents of free trade were equally convinced. We would be more competitive, our exports would increase by leaps and bounds, and with growing prosperity, we would have the confidence in ourselves to be world competitive in the increasingly challenging context of globalization.

Who was right? Only time will tell in a definitive manner. Yet it's possible, ten years later, to examine the results and directions flowing from free trade.

Let put this in context by taking you back 15 years. At one point in the 1980s, the British weekly magazine *The Economist* had carried an editorial headline which read as follows: "Wildcat Canada Resigns from the World." The headline summarized the economic and fiscal policy against which my party, in opposition, waged political battle, culminating in the election of 1984. The reference to "resigning from the world" was a bow to the phenomenon we have come to know as globalization.

This new economic environment is so different, the change so great and the transition to it so wrenching, that some historians compare its impact to that of the Industrial Revolution some 200 years ago. At such a time, people are gripped by anxiety and insecurity. It was no different in the 1980s. A resurgence of protectionist sentiment and policy arose in the Congress of the United States. And as *The Economist* noted, the previous federal government had designed its own Canadian version of Fortress America.

Canada had to alter course. We had to make fundamental policy changes: a Free Trade Agreement with the United States; the NAFTA; abolishing the 13.5 per cent manufacturers' sales tax and introducing a seven per cent consumption tax (the GST) to spur exports; eliminating FIRA; abolishing the National Energy Program, including the PGRT; privatizing Crown assets, from Teleglobe, to Air Canada, to Canadair, and de Havilland to (partially) Petro Canada. The Patent Act was re-vamped to strengthen the pharmaceutical industry and attract billions of dollars in new investment. On the fiscal side, the average rate of growth of programme spending was cut by 70 per cent. Government spending on programmes moved from $1.23 for every dollar in total revenues to $0.97 by 1993. An operating deficit of $16 billion per year was transformed into a $6.6 billion surplus. As a percentage of GDP, the federal deficit was virtually cut in half, from 8.7 per cent in 1984 to 4.6 per cent in 1990–91. The worldwide recession took a serious toll on that number, driving it up to 5.9 per cent, but public finances were still left in a position significantly stronger than where we found them.

The groundwork was laid for a strong, export-driven recovery, which has now come to pass. The day I signed the FTA with President Reagan, exports accounted for approximately 23 per cent of our GDP. Today, that number is over 40 per cent and rising swiftly. By the time my government left office in 1993, the prime rate was at six per cent, the lowest in 20 years; our inflation rate was 1.5 per cent, the lowest in 30 years, and the United Nations had just reported that in terms of quality of life, as you have repeatedly heard, Canada was the number one country in the world. It needs to be emphasized that these policies, whether of free trade or of fiscal management, are not an end in themselves. They are a means to an end, which is the achievement of greater opportunity, higher incomes and better living standards for all Canadians.

Canada and the US are in the vanguard of industrialized nations building a foundation of economic growth and prosperity in which justice and freedom can flourish both at home and around the world.

For generations the United States and Canada have made common cause for both. More than three million jobs in each country depend directly on trade with the other. And that trade has been growing steadily, from both countries, to both countries, since we implemented the Canada–US Free Trade Agreement.

Since the FTA, our exports to the US have skyrocketed by 80 per cent and our total commerce exceeds $1.5 billion per day—almost $600 billion per year—the largest such trade between any two nations in world history.

Canada buys more US products than the fifteen countries in the European Union combined. In fact, the US exports more to Ontario than it does to the nation of Japan. Trade creates jobs—good jobs, high paying jobs, durable jobs. Every $1 billion in trade abroad means approximately 12,000 new jobs at home. And that's what the NAFTA debate has been about —jobs and the future.

At about this time, the new President of Mexico began articulating his vision for the modernization of the Mexican economy. The cornerstone of that great initiative was to be a Free Trade Agreement among Mexico, the United States and Canada. In Mexican terms, the concept was revolutionary and marked a dramatic break with many past policies. In global terms, the concept was unusual in that it marked the first attempt to link, within a free trade zone, the economies of two mature, wealthy, trading countries (both G-7 nations) with that of the equivalent of a developing nation, with relatively limited democratic achievement in terms of politics, public policy, the judiciary and business leadership—when compared with the US or Canada.

NAFTA was successfully negotiated and signed in San Antonio in October 1992, by the Presidents of the United States and Mexico and myself. Based on the Canada–US experience, NAFTA has opened up the Mexican market of 100 million people, creating the largest, richest, single market in the world—400 million people accounting for one-third of the world's output. The future looked brilliant as Mexicans opened their economy for the first time and trade expanded by 25 per cent during the first twelve months. But the enemies of democracy knew that political instability would damage the cause of social justice. I was in Mexico City the day Luis Donaldo Colosio was assassinated. This was an enormous tragedy for Mexico. Later, powerful tragedy struck again, almost suffocating in its wake the great economic advances and structural changes of recent years. In fact Mexicans are beginning to emerge from a period of tremendous anguish— from the peso collapse, to new political assassinations. But because of the strength of the Mexican people and the resolve of their nation, they will survive this and other challenges, and Mexico will pursue a course towards greater democracy, justice and prosperity.

Since the Miami Summit and the decision to expand free trade throughout the hemisphere by 2005, a $13–14 trillion market now awaits North America's entrepreneurs and business community. But, there is a cloud on the horizon. The momentum under American leadership is in the process of being lost. Chile, which was to be the next NAFTA partner, has been stiffed and the pledge of fast track negotiations disappeared in the vapour of election-year politics. President Clinton was in fact denied fast track authority last year by members of his own party in the House of Representatives. As a consequence, Latin American countries are now making major trade deals that exclude the United States.

A customs union known as MERCUSOR has emerged among Brazil, Argentina, Uruguay and Paraguay. Their economies produce almost $2 trillion, 70 per cent of South America's total. In spite of present difficulties, MERCUSOR is prospering. It has signed a free trade agreement with Mexico, is discussing one with Canada, which has just signed an FTA with Chile, and with Europe by the year 2005. This trend away from American leadership is ominous and must be reversed. To handcuff the president of the US at the very moment that international trade sweeps forward as the greatest liberalizing and modernizing force the world has known, is to do an enormous disservice to the US and the goal of increased prosperity and social justice around the world.

And, what of the future? As directed by the Miami and Santiago Summits, work will proceed among the 34 partners and the CBI countries, to achieve "concrete progress" toward the FTAA by the end of 1999. This should include agreements this year on concrete and mutually beneficial business facilitation measures. These could include a code of conduct for customs integrity; improved customs procedures for express shipments; transparency and due process in government procurement; or mutual recognition agreements in the licensed professions.

From there, 2005 will be targeted as the year to complete a rigorous, comprehensive trade agreement, expanding trade, accelerating growth, attracting investment from all over the world and cementing our strategic position in the hemisphere. Its benefits for all of us will be immense. One day, NAFTA's successor—the Free Trade Area of the Americas—shall include 34 countries and 800 million people and the US and Canada will have defined powerful roles for themselves at the very heart of a new free trade zone, stretching from Point Barrow to Patagonia, Hawaii to Recife, Easter Island to Nunavut.

We need to raise living standards. Families will benefit from a wider availability of goods and services, with better quality and lower prices.

Domestic firms in each FTAA member country will become more efficient as they more easily import capital and informatics goods—and employ the higher technologies that become available when intellectual property protection improves. We should encourage competition, transparency, and impartial regulation in, and continued deregulation of, the service industries—financial systems, telecommunications, insurance, construction, the professions and more. We should develop enhanced means of resolving trade disputes. We should become more effective in addressing our... Finally, we will strengthen the values of openness, accountability, and democracy which themselves make the FTAA possible.

Canada's economy has undergone massive restructuring and modernizing over the last dozen years. The results are evident and persuasive. We are growing into a competitive country whose lifeline is exports and international trade. This new growth and wealth have enabled us to eliminate the deficits—both provincially and federally—and begin the process of paying down our debt, while cutting taxes in some jurisdictions for our citizens. The controversial and painful measures introduced to achieve this—principally the trilogy of free trade, GST and high interest rates to eliminate inflation—have clearly made us stronger and enabled Canada to dramatically improve the state of our public finances.

This new economic strength has in turn significantly enhanced Canadian sovereignty—because such sovereignty is merely an illusion without the financial clout to back it up and the economic opportunity it offers to growing numbers of our citizens.

Canada, like other privileged nations, is often extremely resistant to change. Deep and important structural changes are indispensable, however, to maintain a growing economy and can only be brought about by a firm expression of political will. For a generation raised on the bizarre proposition that leadership should be equated with popularity, measured and published weekly, this can be a daunting challenge. In fact "transforming leadership"—leadership that makes a significant difference in the life of a nation—recognizes that political capital is acquired to be spent in great causes for one's country.

Prime ministers are not chosen to seek popularity. They are chosen to provide leadership. There are times when Canadians must be told not what they want to hear, but what they have to know. And what they have to know is a quotation from the Book of Proverbs inscribed on the Peace Tower in Ottawa: "Where there is no vision, the people perish."

Leaders must have vision and they must find the courage to fight for the policies that will give that vision life. Leaders must govern not for easy headlines in ten days but for a better Canada in ten years—and they must be ready to endure the attacks and the opprobrium that often accompany profound or controversial change, while they await the distant and compelling sounds of a verdict that only history and a more reflective nation can render in the fullness of time.

It was a great and genuine privilege to serve as prime minister at a time of remarkable challenge and convulsive change, at home and around the world. Many of you here today participated in that journey in differing ways, for which I express deep gratitude and personal admiration. The service of one's country is the noblest one of all.

Democracies are inspired by the collision of great ideas and the vigorous disagreements and debates they provoke. In this great debate all the participants from all parties and all parts of the political spectrum—in government or out—have served Canada well, and I feel honoured to be in your company.

Notes for Remarks by President George Bush
NAFTA: The Tenth Anniversary
Washington, D.C.
9 December 2002

Of course, it is a special joy to be here with my former colleagues from the world stage—two men with whom I was proud to work on some tough, forward-looking issues, and hopefully make a difference. Winston Churchill once noted he did not fear how history would treat him, for he planned to write that history himself. You can't be a president or a prime minister without some appreciation for the sweep of history, and I have no doubt that when the history of our time together is finally written, it will be recorded that Prime Minister Mulroney and President Salinas led their proud countries with exceptional talent and distinction.

And while I am not sure what I can add to what they have already observed about "NAFTA at Ten", I am happy to share a few thoughts about this watershed moment not only in American history, but in the history of North America, when we decided we would seek progress—to step forward —together.

For starters, when I look back at the events of ten years ago, it is with a mixture of great pride—but also some reticence. I say this because in December of 1992, remember, I had just received what Churchill called the "Order of the Boot"—having lost the election, fair and square, to President Clinton.

So in a personal sense, you might say I was coming to terms with my own political mortality—and preparing to transition to what has now been a thoroughly fulfilling, full, active, and very happy retirement.

But there were two main items of unfinished business to tend to before being sworn out of Office—one of them being the START II agreement I signed in Moscow in January of 1993 with President Yeltsin to drastically reduce the nuclear arsenals maintained by the two superpowers and, thus, also drastically reduce the threat of nuclear war.

But preceding START II by a few weeks, right here in Washington, was the signing of NAFTA. As we know now, the agreement we signed 10 years ago created the largest, richest, and most productive market in the world.

It was an extraordinary achievement; and appropriately, since NAFTA was a cornerstone for expanding trade within the Western Hemisphere, we signed the accord at the Organization of American States. This was symbolically important because, among other things, we wanted to use economic reform as a vehicle for peaceful resolution of the conflicts in Central America. Just as important: We wanted to achieve progress on Latin American development issues while solidifying closer ties among […] our trusted Canadian and Mexican neighbours.

When I came into Office in 1989 after eight years at Ronald Reagan's side, I was already a firm believer that trade and investment were the only way to improve the collective economic prospects of the hemisphere. In short, it was the only road—the proven road—to the future we all wanted to see realized. And to this end, to fully engage our Central and South American neighbors on a broad range of issues from debt relief to trade and investment accords, our team launched the Enterprise for the Americas Initiative in 1990.

When it later came to negotiating NAFTA, of course, we—Brian, Carlos, and I—knew it wouldn't be easy. On several occasions, Brian has referred to the fact that at certain points his political support was down to members of his immediate family, and I know how he feels.

But we stayed the course, because in the end we believed that economic reform would contribute to increased political stability and democracy in the Western Hemisphere. We believed that not only would trade benefit our neighbours, it would open new markets—new opportunities—for tens of millions of businesses and investors.

Perhaps that is why signing the NAFTA agreement was one of my proudest moments as president of the United States. I viewed the agreement as a concrete and constructive step forward to greater prosperity and stability across the region.

And here I want to acknowledge the exceptional efforts of US negotiators Bob Mosbacher, Carla Hills and Jules Katz, as well as their outstanding counterparts Jaime Serra and Michael Wilson and their respective colleagues. They and their superb teams did a marvelous job in concluding these complicated talks in a little over one year.

I want to stress that many individuals beyond these top negotiators worked diligently for the success of NAFTA. In the United States, many in both parties labored on behalf of NAFTA. I am grateful for their hard work.

I also want to salute former President Bill Clinton for fighting for NAFTA after I left the White House. I appreciate what he and his administration did in getting the accord through Congress with the help of a lot of congressional Republicans. They lobbied tirelessly on behalf of the agreement because it was right for our country—and right for our hemisphere.

Of course, as we have heard, achieving NAFTA was not easy. There were opponents across the political spectrum in each of our three nations.

In particular, I remember reference being made to a "sucking sound" of Americans jobs going out of the country; but, again, we stayed the course, because we knew that in the end more trade would yield results—including, for the record, millions of new, higher-paying jobs. True, I read a report that, in 1997, the US lost some 385,000 manufacturing jobs; but at the same time, we added more than three million jobs in advanced sectors such as computer programming and management consulting.

So there is a trade-off in some ways—a painful trade-off for many, but one I believe we simply must endure if we want to position America to compete for, and win, new business in this increasingly interconnected and competitive global economy.

Now, am I happy that 385,000 Americans lost manufacturing jobs in 1997? No, not for a second. Many of them had families to feed, but the argument is that adding millions of better paying jobs to the rolls benefits us all in the long run. And the two million NAFTA-related jobs that have been created in the US since 1993 pay between 13 and 18 per cent more than the average national wage.

And as we have already heard Brian and Carlos describe in detail, NAFTA isn't just a two-way street, it's a three way street. The Foreign Direct Investment inflows into the NAFTA countries between 1994 and 2000 reached $1.3 trillion—or about 28 per cent of the world total. Of this, a Dow Jones report out just last week noted that 70 per cent of the FDI into Mexico has come from the United States. (Maybe some of you saw this, but the Bancomext director put out a release last Wednesday citing the 13,715 Mexican companies that have received American investment since NAFTA was signed.)

Now, I know many of you are in for two intensive days of examining this Agreement and the complex details that go along with it—and so, in a kinder and gentler way, I do not want to bludgeon anyone to death with statistics.

But I know part of the agenda for this conference is to examine the prospects of the Doha Development Round, and several panels will look at what it takes to "get globalization right". So let me just broaden the perspective here for a just a moment.

If you look around the world, freer trade has clearly delivered benefits to developing countries as well. For example, as a recent IMF paper points out, in trade-opening East Asian countries—the so-called "New Globalizers" —the number of people in absolute poverty declined by over 120 million between 1993 and 1998.

Moreover, since the Seattle WTO meeting, governments comprising about a quarter of the world's total population—some 1.5 billion people— have joined the WTO. And another two dozen or so countries are currently negotiating their terms of membership, perhaps most significantly Russia. The WTO's multilateral trading system is now nearly universal, covering more than 97 per cent of total global trade.

This is a positive development in my view. Some experts predict that, by 2015, reshaping the world's trading system and reducing barriers to trade in goods could reduce the number of poor people in developing countries by 300 million—and boost global income by as much as $2.8 trillion over the next decade.

Of course, in many political corners, including here in the US, trade will continue to stir up parochial passions. The process of advancing the trade agenda often involves several steps forward, as we witnessed 10 years ago, followed by occasional steps backwards—as we saw in Seattle in 1999, where a lawless mob of anarchists showed the world their true, extreme colors.

Extremists like that either don't "get" the benefits of freer and fairer trade, or are simply content to ignore the facts. One problem, as WTO

Director Mike Moore has noted, is that the "anti-globalization (movement) is confused with anti-Americanism. Little credit is given to the fact that US companies account for around one-fifth of total world imports, and almost one-quarter of total exports."

But we are also aware that 96 per cent of the world's consumers live outside the US, and that the more prosperous they become, the better it is for US businesses.

Is the current system perfect? Far from it. No country adheres to totally free trade. Every country finds that it has to compromise from time to time. Sometimes it is agriculture; sometimes it is textiles; sometimes it's steel imports.

Those of us who support more trade must acknowledge that managing trade relations is on-going work, and FTA and NAFTA were just a starting point in an ever-evolving process of balancing competing objectives between the increasing numbers of nations who seek genuine, sustainable progress for their peoples.

I believe that, given time, the Administration, the Congress, the WTO, and the other participants responsible for designing and managing the system of global trade will iron out differences that emerge and identify certain fundamental principles that govern the way we trade products. For example, we must be sure to avoid having regional trading pacts turn inward, and evolve into protectionist "blocks". In my view, agreements like NAFTA and MECOSUR should be but steps to knocking down more barriers and joining more nation and regions together.

And I am heartened that, in the US, the Congress passed Trade Promotion Authority legislation empowering the President to strike more trade deals with our hemispheric partners vis-à-vis the FTAA. With some 22 million jobs in the US depending on trade, now is not the time to rest on our laurels. This hemispheric FTAA agreement uniting the Americas in free trade would link 34 countries with 800 million people producing roughly $13 trillion in goods and services.

Indeed, the benefits of free trade would seem clear, and yet, some remain oblivious to the magic and resilience of opening more markets. At precisely the moment history beckons us to take wing—and realize the promise of a new world order in which ideas and commerce are more freely exchanged throughout the global village—some seem intent on sticking their collective heads in the sand.

Speaking for my own country, we simply cannot retreat from the world; we cannot withdraw into a "Fortress America"; we cannot give in to the selfish voices of isolation and the timid voices of protectionism.

Having said that, I feel obliged to warn you that, at this stage of my life, I don't normally "do" issues. But this NAFTA issue is near and dear to my heart—enough for me to come to Washington, where I do not often visit. That surprises some people, I guess, but it's true.

We only have one President at a time. Almost ten years ago, I promised President Clinton that I would try very hard not to criticize or second-guess him in public, understanding that he had a very big job to do and that there were plenty able men and women in the loyal opposition to battle for the principles I share.

I have worked very hard to extend the same courtesy to the 43rd President... but all bets are off with Barbara... As the President has noted, I give him advice when he asks for it, and his mother gives advice even when he doesn't ask...

No, I had my chance, and did my best. As LBJ said of his time in office: "I lived thoroughly every hour... I had known sorrow and anger, frustration and disappointment, pain and dismay. But more than anything else, I experienced the towering pride and pleasure at having had my chance to make my contribution to solving the problems of our times..."

Thomas Jefferson once said that "there comes a time when men should go, and not occupy too long the high ground to which others have the right to advance." And so it is in the Bush family.

I am honored to be here at this prestigious institution along with my two former colleagues for whom I have great affection.

Notes For An Address
By The Right Honourable Brian Mulroney
NAFTA At 10:
Progress, Potential and Precedents
Washington, D.C.
9 December 2002

Exactly one month after my birth, Winston Churchill described the Canadian-American relationship in memorable terms: "That long frontier from the Atlantic to the Pacific oceans, guarded only by neighbourly respect and honourable obligations, is an example to every country and a pattern for the future of the world". In the 63 years since Churchill spoke, neither of our countries has done anything to diminish the expectations of excellence and cooperation he forecast.

For Canada and the United States, the post-Cold War world offers unique opportunities and daunting challenges. We begin from a common heritage of democratic traditions and a defence of liberty. There are reminders of that from the trenches of one war to the beaches of the next, places inscribed in the history of valour, where Canadians and Americans have fought together, where Canadians and Americans have died together, in the defence of freedom.

It was on the basis of these shared values and common achievements that, as a new Prime Minister in 1985, I signaled President Reagan that Canada was interested in negotiating a comprehensive free trade agreement with the United States of America. I was aware that similar attempts by Canadian Prime Ministers had foundered painfully over the previous 100 years, in large measure because of a reality described by Prime Minister and Nobel Laureate Lester B. Pearson:

> The picture of weak and timid Canadian negotiators being pushed around and brow-beaten by American representatives into settlements that were "sell-outs" is a false and distorted one. It is often painted, however, by Canadians who think that a sure way to get applause and support at home is to exploit our anxieties and exaggerate our suspicions over US power and policies.

I knew we would have to confront a powerful American administration at the bargaining table and an influential clutch of naysayers at home. The fact that the US population base and economic power was roughly 10 times ours did nothing to soften my critics' charges that, if successful, this would make Canada the 51st state. At that time, access to our most important market was being threatened. A severe wave of protectionism swept through Congress like a bitter November wind and about 40 per cent of our exports to the United States were subject to quotas, "voluntary" restraints and other restrictions. As I indicated to the House of Commons, by way of illustration of the mood and atmosphere that existed in the United States, the Ottinger Bill, passed three successive years by the House of Representatives, sought to destroy the Auto Pact, the heart of Ontario's economic power in Canada. The Americans also demanded punitive action against Canadian lumber, steel, uranium, cement, subway cars, and fish, in fact virtually all of our exports.

There was a crisis a month for one Canadian exporter after another, as new trade barriers were erected against Canadian products and new legal interpretations were advanced to inhibit Canadian access to the US market. That is the challenge we faced at that time and I believed the negotiation of a bold new trade agreement offered the most realistic solution on behalf of the people of Canada.

In 1987, following more than two years of difficult negotiations, we reached agreement. President Reagan and I subsequently signed the massive and quite radical agreement, which came into effect on 1 January 1989. In Canada, we had to endure a vicious three-year onslaught and unprecedented vitriolic personal attack—and I had to call and win a brutal general election campaign—before we could enact the agreement into law. According to our opponents it was going to be an unrelieved disaster and Canada was going to lose its shirt. So what happened?

Well, last year, two-way trade in goods and services between our countries exploded to $700 billion. It is now $2 billion a day, more than $1.3 million per minute, every day of the year, the largest amount of commerce between any two nations in world history. Canada is the number one export market for 37 of the American states, and Canada buys more goods from the United States than the 15 countries of the EU combined. America now exports three times as much to Canada as to China, Hong Kong and Taiwan combined. The value of goods crossing the Windsor-Detroit border point alone is greater than total United States trade with Japan. Investment has grown along with trade. As Canada's exports to its NAFTA partners increased 95 per cent from 1993 to 2001, average annual FDI inflows averaged $21.4 billion during the same period, four times the average of the seven years prior to NAFTA.

And trade means jobs. Approximately four new jobs in five in Canada have been created by trade since 1993, the year the present government took office. The first act in a visionary hemispheric trade trilogy was now complete, made possible throughout the process by the exceptional friendship and support towards Canada of President Reagan and Vice President Bush.

A little later, the new President of Mexico, Carlos Salinas, began articulating his impressive programme for the modernization of the Mexican economy. The cornerstone of that great initiative was to be a Free Trade Agreement between Mexico, the United States and Canada. In Mexican terms, the concept was revolutionary and marked a dramatic break with many past policies. In global terms, the concept was unusual in that it marked the first attempt to link, within a free trade zone, the economies of two mature, wealthy, trading countries (both G-7 nations) with that of the equivalent of a developing nation, with relatively limited democratic achievement in terms of politics, public policy, the judiciary and business leadership—when compared with the US or Canada.

Fortunately, the White House was occupied by President George H.W. Bush, a visionary leader, whose skills would end the Cold War and ignite the tremendous promise of a dramatic new reach into Mexico and Latin America, bringing stability and prosperity in its wake. The negotiations were arduous, complex and challenging. In spite of the political risks, the three leaders envisioned the long-term benefits and NAFTA was successfully concluded and signed in San Antonio in October 1992 by President Bush of the United States, President Salinas of Mexico and myself.

In all of our countries, some leaders from other parties supported us all. I know that the indispensable leadership of President Bush was later supplemented by the efforts of Mac McLarty, Richard Fisher and many others in the new Clinton administration, under the direction of the President, to ensure passage of the NAFTA legislation. Based on the Canada–US experience, NAFTA has opened up the Mexican market of 100 million people, creating the largest, richest, single market in the world—400 million people accounting for one-third of the world's output, approximately $11 trillion per year.

This constituted the second act in the trilogy.

Mexico's exports have increased by over 220 per cent between 1993 and 2001 and Mexico's average annual capital inflow has reached almost $12 billion, three times the annual amount in the seven years prior to NAFTA. As a result, since NAFTA, Mexico has now surpassed Japan as America's number two trading partner even though its economy is one-twelfth the size of Japan's.

The rise of trade between Mexico and Canada, countries with modest economic links prior to NAFTA, was dramatic, and is now worth more than $10 billion a year, our sixth largest trade partner. The fear mongering of those who predicted massive losses of jobs, the curtailing of sovereignty, a race to the bottom in environmental and social policy have all proved hollow. Our countries are stronger, our economies more robust, our peoples more prosperous, our social structures more resilient, our capital markets more stable, our roles in the world more vigorous as a result of NAFTA.

We have, in short, accomplished much. There are, however, new challenges that face us and opportunities open to us as we try to manage an intensifying economic relationship and cope with increasing threats to our shared values and security. These issues are inseparable. North America is more than a free trade area. It is a community of values motivated by a deep belief in democracy, economic opportunity, tolerance and the rule of law. It is three countries sharing a critical infrastructure of pipelines, telecommunication networks, rail and power lines. It is three closely integrated economies whose prosperity depends on free flows of people and goods between them.

It is, in short, an area whose social, economic and national security is indivisible. Our economic security relies on seamless borders within North America. Our security against global terrorism and criminality can only be ensured by acting together to protect our external borders, before threats can reach any of our territories. Our values are only safe if we insist on practicing them and make them a compelling example to the world. It is essential therefore that we dedicate ourselves to protecting our shared continent together and to work together in the world, acting in defence of our beliefs.

Let me list some of the tasks I see lying ahead for us in North America. First and foremost, the NAFTA partners must dedicate themselves as a matter of the greatest urgency to building an area of security in North America, one that denies terrorism a foothold on our continent and ensures uninterrupted legitimate flows among us. Such common action is also essential to allow us to protect the great North/South flows of goods, people, technology that underpins our shared prosperity. Our internal borders will only be smart if our external perimeter is secure. We may well need new political institutions (Ministerial Councils) to heighten vigilance and direct concrete action which gives all of North America more certainty against the unprecedented threat of terrorism. We must make our internal borders work in our shared interest rather than succumbing to the false temptation of sealing them off against each other to protect security. Doing so would be a victory for terrorists.

We must also protect our shared economic security against political expediency. An economic relationship that is so close and so strongly based in mutual reliance, should not be subject to the misuse of draconian trade instruments. The sometimes arbitrary application of trade remedies in North America can have the most hurtful consequences on communities and on whole regions in our countries. They serve no one but special interests and hurt consumers.

Though the application of such measures has fallen significantly since the conclusion of NAFTA, each instance is like a violent lurch in a stable relationship, a rude assault on the fundamental goals of a grand continental partnership. In my view, we should press for a common standard of trade remedy embracing the rule of law rather than the rule of power. There are other more effective means to resolve our trade disputes, such as appeals under what are highly compatible national competition laws. We should, in any event, rely on and reinforce our shared mechanisms to resolve disputes. These have worked well; made more permanent and properly resourced, they could perform even better.

Also important to our shared welfare in North America is the flow of services, technology and knowledge. These are conveyed by people. Assuring their movement across our borders should be the focus of renewed attention as we put in place the new structures we need to protect our security. Our economies are now closely connected and interdependent, a reality that needs to be better reflected in the way our governments manage our national affairs and in the way they regulate economic activity. They should work together to ensure that while our national systems of regulation serve to protect our citizens, and are fully respectful of our different constitutions, they are also as compatible as possible in order to increase the efficiency of our economies and enhance our global competitiveness.

The future is also full of possibility for achieving a closer sense of community among our three countries—through education, culture, shared infrastructure and the collaboration between local communities. Our governments should also engage more vigorously in the effort to define a vision that will benefit all our peoples, a vision of a vibrant harmonious continent. It is therefore vital that the third act in the trilogy now be completed. After a decade of tremendous progress towards democracy throughout Latin America, uncertainty and unpredictability are now creeping into fragile democratic institutions from Venezuela to Brazil to Argentina.

They must now be drawn together into greater prosperity and deeper democracy by a powerful act of political leadership. If this occurs, one day, NAFTA's successor—the Free Trade Area of the Americas—shall include 34 countries and 800 million people with an annual GDP of $12.5 trillion and the US, Canada and Mexico will have defined a powerful role for themselves at the very heart of a new free trade zone, stretching from Montreal to Monterrey, Point Barrow to Patagonia, Hawaii to Honduras, Easter Island to Nunavut. The geopolitical and international security implications of this new grouping will be profoundly beneficial for us all.

NAFTA is about more than North America. We are countries of the Americas. I say this proudly as the leader of the Government which made Canada a member of the Organization of American States in 1990. Canada's decision to join the OAS was a historic one reversing long-standing Canadian policy and based in our confidence that we were at home in the region, that democracy and respect for human rights was embedded in the Hemisphere, that the countries of the Americas were committed to the rule of law and open economies. The decision was a prelude to Canada's finally assuming a leadership role in its own hemisphere.

Led by wealthy and powerful G-7 nations—the US and Canada—societies that understand free trade agreements must initially allow poorer economies to prosper quickly—the democracies of the Hemisphere are now committed to social equity, freer markets, less state intervention and a firmer rule of law.

They want to reap the advantages that these offer their societies, but all agree that free trade, particularly access to the great markets of NAFTA and Brazil will be essential if they are to be able to do so. That is why the countries of the Hemisphere, inspired by the vision first articulated by

President Reagan, agreed to a Free Trade Area of the Americas. President Bush carried forward that vision in his powerful Enterprise for the Americas initiative in 1990 and the leaders of the Hemisphere launched the FTAA negotiations four years later.

Our governments have agreed to conclude the FTAA by 2005, a little over two years from now. Much hard negotiation lies ahead. Some countries of the Americas have made confident strides towards open economies, but a number have stumbled and others face difficult political and social choices. The prospect of a successful FTAA agreement is the strongest support for their efforts that we could give them. It has the capacity to change their lives in dramatic fashion and forever.

It is our privilege, in North America, to have made a success of free trade. It is now our responsibility to share that success. The Americas are our neighbourhood. Our security depends on our neighbours' capacity to provide stability under the effective rule of law. Our prosperity will be enhanced as theirs is assumed.

The FTAA negotiations are at a critical stage. We have the opportunity, as the United States and Brazil assume chairmanship of the process, to make them a historic success. We must not underestimate the complexity of the task, particularly given that the global negotiations on new WTO rules are also under way. Nor should we forget that the countries of the Americas are pursuing two linked goals: democracy and economic growth. The leaders of the Americas agreed at the Quebec City Summit last year on the bond between the freedom to trade and the freedom to enjoy democratic institutions. It is important, in my view, that the FTAA re-assert it to underline that freedom —economic and political—is indivisible. The agreement should provide that the benefits of free trade are open only to democracies living under the rule of law and with respect for human rights.

What then are some of the key issues to resolve if the FTAA is to become reality? One is the need to guarantee access to our markets for the exports that matter most for our partners, particularly the export of agricultural commodities. This ought to be the first step on "the ladder of economic prosperity" that poor countries desperately seek to take. But the rich countries pay out more than $300 billion a year in farm subsidies, thereby enabling farmers in some industrialized countries to sell overseas at 20 per cent below the actual cost of production, and consequently killing off any hope for developing countries to compete effectively. Just to be sure, in the US there are further tariff barriers that make it doubly tough for many third world farmers to sell any of their produce here at all.

We will, in turn, need to be assured that their markets are open to us, particularly to the provision of services by North American suppliers, whose participation will bring innovation and efficiency in their wake. The agreement should provide rules that protect the rights of foreign investors against arbitrary and discriminatory action. The agreement should establish effective mechanisms to resolve disputes among us. The NAFTA and the WTO provide rich experience on which to draw to make such a system both responsive and authoritative. The agreement should provide for the movement of people, allowing professionals much greater freedom to provide services across the region, students to benefit from a wider range of learning opportunities, and our citizens to share in the great cultural gifts of our Hemisphere. The freedom of movement, across our borders, both of goods and people is elemental to the notion of free trade. In the world of the twenty-first century, however, such a freedom must not be left open to abuse. It must be accompanied by agreements to eliminate threats to our security, whether from global criminality or its Siamese twin—global terrorism. The commitment to fight the illegal traffic in people, drugs and capital must be intensified as part of our efforts to build a community based on free trade in the Hemisphere.

Lastly, countries of the FTAA should establish fora where environmental and labour issues can be studied and reviewed among our governments, where best practices can be shared and where those who do not honour their own laws respecting these matters can be held to account by their peers. The agenda I have sketched here is ambitious. Some will say it is unattainable. But the remarkable thing about the FTA and NAFTA is that success emerged despite heavy obstacles and fierce opposition. The leadership and perseverance that forged those agreements are paying dividends today for all three partners. The power of a good idea should never be underestimated. It could happen again. It should happen again.

We who have benefited so dramatically from a decade of free trade in North America have a special role to play. We are able to offer our success as an example of what is possible. Access to our markets will be critical to assuring stability and growth in our sister democracies now passing through a period of uncertainty, sometimes of stagnation and turmoil. NAFTA's place will evolve, depending on the outcome of these trade negotiations. It will continue to be a critical bond among the countries of North America; its importance in the Hemisphere as an example is unquestioned; its role as a magnet will be compelling.

Ten years on, there is much to celebrate in what we North Americans have accomplished. Ten years from today, however, we must gather again to celebrate the great achievement of a new generation of political leaders: the binding together of all peoples and countries of the western hemisphere who believe in freedom and practice democracy in a vast free trade zone, greater than the world has ever before seen, which will ensure growing prosperity and durable social justice for many, long deprived of both. And in the process, we will contribute to the political stability and peaceful progress for all peoples, becoming, as Churchill predicted, a model for all mankind.

Brian Mulroney
A New World Order
Bush Presidential Library
College Station, Texas
20 October 2003

As we know, our world has changed, perhaps forever, because a handful of terrorists flew planes into American landmarks on a beautiful Tuesday morning, killing innocent men, women and children. Now, the overriding predicate of US policy—foreign, defence, security, domestic—is to ensure this never happens again.

It is out of these new realities that the doctrine of unilateral pre-emption, so condemned by many allies, has emerged. I believe an accurate translation of the doctrine is: If the US has persuasive evidence that a country is either contemplating an attack on the US or its allies or harbouring terrorists who might strike out at the US, or its allies around the globe, then the US will—with Security Council approval or without—pre-emptively act to remove the offending government from office.

Why is this doctrine so offensive to so many? Some fear the precedent, others the erosion of multilateralism, and others still a negative impact on the United Nations. As a committed multilateralist and UN supporter, I'm not offended. But Washington alone cannot define when pre-emptive action is necessary; rather, it could display a high degree of statesmanship by initiating a serious dialogue with the permanent five UN Security Council members about appropriate conditions and limitations on its use.

The historical record shows that Security Council approval has never been a sacrosanct pre-condition to action against a hostile state. In fact, a coalition including France, Germany and Canada mounted a massive air war against Serbia without Security Council authorization, under President Bill Clinton's leadership. Serbia did not represent a threat to anyone outside its own borders. Why the reversal of policy when Iraq was involved, with the same nations piously insisting that Security Council approval had to be obtained before any military action?

President George W. Bush hasn't been the only leader to contemplate pre-emption as a policy; 12 years ago at Stanford University convocation, I stated that Canada favoured "rethinking the limits of national sovereignty in a world where problems respect no borders. Just a few days ago, Iraq blocked a UN arms inspection on grounds of national sovereignty. In the past year, countries have blocked food delivery to starving people, again on grounds of national sovereignty... Quite frankly, such invocations of the principle of national sovereignty are as offensive to me as the police declining to stop family violence [in the belief that] a man's home is his castle. We must recognize that there are certain fundamental rights... and that, sometimes, the international community must act to defend them."

Now, I am not a proponent of naked unilateralism. Leadership does not equate with unilateralism; nor does it imply a unipolar world, which would be unstable. Burden-sharing requires decision-sharing. The burden of building a new, sensible world order must be shared by all industrialized nations.

It is obvious that the US and UK-led alliance is now in serious difficulty in Iraq. The quality of planning for the invasion clearly surpassed that of the occupation. But Mr. Bush cannot, will not and should not walk away from Iraq.

In my opinion, America now greatly needs international allies who can re-establish a basis of mutual trust and candour. True allies must now come to the assistance of the US-led alliance by showing flexibility and co-operation both at the UN and on the ground in Iraq.

Since the collapse of the former Soviet Union, the United States and it allies have struggled to establish a New World Order. Some problems have worsened. The North Korean threat is more acute, but may elicit more constructive involvement from Japan and an economically ascendant China, which is redefining its global role. Africa is slipping further into despotism and devastation.

Still, the gravest threat to global stability is terrorism. In a war on terror, the more extended US resources become, the more vulnerable they are to attack, ambush and hostage-taking. History demonstrates that democracies have limited staying power for long, drawn-out, inconclusive struggles, no matter how noble the desire to do good.

To be effective, power depends ultimately on the will of those who possess it to sustain it. As the sole global powerhouse, the US is a frustrated superpower, hesitant to assume single-handedly the burdens of a twenty-first century Rome. The gravest risk of all would be a retreat by the US into a new strain of isolationism.

What is needed to retain both the Americans' leadership and their full engagement? A new sense of partnership with nations holding similar values. After all, terrorists can strike from Tokyo to Toronto.

Canadians, Europeans and others share American commitments to democracy, human rights and the basic tenets of economic liberalization. For too long have we reduced our capacity and our inclination for self-defence. We must redefine our roles and responsibilities in the aftermath of war in Iraq and Afghanistan and develop a more concerted game plan to confront terrorism globally.

It was 58 years ago that statesmen from around the world gathered in San Francisco to draft the UN Charter. The UN has been an imperfect but often effective instrument of peace. The successful execution of the UN Security Council mandate in the 1991 Persian Gulf War was a giant step in the right direction.

But the UN is like a sheriff without a police force, unable to respond efficiently or effectively to global conflict, even genocide, constrained by decision-making structures which were designed for a different age, with little regard to compliance with its own principles and resolutions. Thus, Iraq under Saddam Hussein was chosen to preside over disarmament affairs, while Libya chairs the UN Committee on Human Rights!

History tells us that international institutions which fail to act in the face of global crises wither away. Reform is therefore essential. To help maintain world order, the UN needs a decision-making structure that works—and resources to give force to its resolutions.

In my judgement, the US should instigate and lead San Francisco II, a major reform effort to establish new multilateral approaches that respect the basic principles of the UN Charter. It is vital for Canada and the world that the US remains fully engaged as the bulwark for multilateralism.

Without US engagement, there can be no effective multilateral effort. But, without close support and unvarnished counsel from its key allies, the US will inevitably exercise its own will. Only the US and her allies have the unique combination of vast economic strength, extraordinary military power and a history of willingness to assume burdens in the defence of freedom.

Queen's Policy Studies
Recent Publications

The Queen's Policy Studies Series is dedicated to the exploration of major public policy issues that confront governments and society in Canada and other nations.

Our books are available from good bookstores everywhere, including the Queen's University bookstore (http://www.campusbookstore.com/). McGill-Queen's University Press is the exclusive world representative and distributor of books in the series. A full catalogue and ordering information may be found on their web site (http://mqup.mcgill.ca/).

School of Policy Studies

Measuring What Matters in Peace Operations and Crisis Management, Sarah Jane Meharg, 2009. Paper 978-1-55339-228-6 Cloth ISBN 978-1-55339-229-3

International Migration and the Governance of Religious Diversity, Paul Bramadat and Matthias Koenig (eds.), 2009. Paper 978-1-55339-266-8 Cloth ISBN 978-1-55339-267-5

Who Goes? Who Stays? What Matters? Accessing and Persisting in Post-Secondary Education in Canada, Ross Finnie, Richard E. Mueller, Arthur Sweetman, and Alex Usher (eds.), 2008. Paper 978-1-55339-221-7 Cloth ISBN 978-1-55339-222-4

Economic Transitions with Chinese Characteristics: Thirty Years of Reform and Opening Up, Arthur Sweetman and Jun Zhang (eds.), 2009
Paper 978-1-55339-225-5 Cloth ISBN 978-1-55339-226-2

Economic Transitions with Chinese Characteristics: Social Change During Thirty Years of Reform, Arthur Sweetman and Jun Zhang (eds.), 2009
Paper 978-1-55339-234-7 Cloth ISBN 978-1-55339-235-4

Dear Gladys: Letters from Over There, Gladys Osmond (Gilbert Penney ed.), 2009
Paper ISBN 978-1-55339-223-1

Immigration and Integration in Canada in the Twenty-first Century, John Biles, Meyer Burstein, and James Frideres (eds.), 2008
Paper ISBN 978-1-55339-216-3 Cloth ISBN 978-1-55339-217-0

Robert Stanfield's Canada, Richard Clippingdale, 2008   ISBN 978-1-55339-218-7

Exploring Social Insurance: Can a Dose of Europe Cure Canadian Health Care Finance? Colleen Flood, Mark Stabile, and Carolyn Tuohy (eds.), 2008
Paper ISBN 978-1-55339-136-4 Cloth ISBN 978-1-55339-213-2

Canada in NORAD, 1957–2007: A History, Joseph T. Jockel, 2007.
Paper ISBN 978-1-55339-134-0 Cloth ISBN 978-1-55339-135-7

Canadian Public-Sector Financial Management, Andrew Graham, 2007
Paper ISBN 978-1-55339-120-3 Cloth ISBN 978-1-55339-121-0

Emerging Approaches to Chronic Disease Management in Primary Health Care,
John Dorland and Mary Ann McColl (eds.), 2007
Paper ISBN 978-1-55339-130-2 Cloth ISBN 978-1-55339-131-9

Fulfilling Potential, Creating Success: Perspectives on Human Capital Development,
Garnett Picot, Ron Saunders and Arthur Sweetman (eds.), 2007
Paper ISBN 978-1-55339-127-2 Cloth ISBN 978-1-55339-128-9

Reinventing Canadian Defence Procurement: A View from the Inside, Alan S. Williams,
2006 Paper ISBN 0-9781693-0-1 (Published in association with Breakout Educational
Network)

SARS in Context: Memory, History, Policy, Jacalyn Duffin and Arthur Sweetman (eds.),
2006 Paper ISBN 978-0-7735-3194-9 Cloth ISBN 978-0-7735-3193-2
(Published in association with McGill-Queen's University Press)

Dreamland: How Canada's Pretend Foreign Policy has Undermined Sovereignty, Roy
Rempel, 2006 Paper ISBN 1-55339-118-7 Cloth ISBN 1-55339-119-5
(Published in association with Breakout Educational Network)

Canadian and Mexican Security in the New North America: Challenges and Prospects,
Jordi Díez (ed.), 2006
Paper ISBN 978-1-55339-123-4 Cloth ISBN 978-1-55339-122-7

*Global Networks and Local Linkages: The Paradox of Cluster Development in an Open
Economy*, David A. Wolfe and Matthew Lucas (eds.), 2005
Paper ISBN 1-55339-047-4 Cloth ISBN 1-55339-048-2

Choice of Force: Special Operations for Canada, David Last and Bernd Horn (eds.),
2005 Paper ISBN 1-55339-044-X Cloth ISBN 1-55339-045-8

Force of Choice: Perspectives on Special Operations, Bernd Horn, J. Paul de B. Taillon,
and David Last (eds.), 2004   Paper ISBN 1-55339-042-3 Cloth 1-55339-043-1

New Missions, Old Problems, Douglas L. Bland, David Last, Franklin Pinch, and Alan
Okros (eds.), 2004   Paper ISBN 1-55339-034-2 Cloth 1-55339-035-0

*The North American Democratic Peace: Absence of War and Security Institution-Build-
ing in Canada-US Relations*, 1867-1958, Stéphane Roussel, 2004
Paper ISBN 0-88911-937-6 Cloth 0-88911-932-2

Implementing Primary Care Reform: Barriers and Facilitators, Ruth Wilson, S.E.D.
Shortt and John Dorland (eds.), 2004
Paper ISBN 1-55339-040-7 Cloth 1-55339-041-5

Social and Cultural Change, David Last, Franklin Pinch, Douglas L. Bland, and
Alan Okros (eds.), 2004   Paper ISBN 1-55339-032-6 Cloth 1-55339-033-4

Clusters in a Cold Climate: Innovation Dynamics in a Diverse Economy, David A.
Wolfe and Matthew Lucas (eds.), 2004
Paper ISBN 1-55339-038-5 Cloth 1-55339-039-3

Canada Without Armed Forces? Douglas L. Bland (ed.), 2004
Paper ISBN 1-55339-036-9 Cloth 1-55339-037-7

*Campaigns for International Security: Canada's Defence Policy at the Turn of the
Century*, Douglas L. Bland and Sean M. Maloney, 2004
Paper ISBN 0-88911-962-7 Cloth 0-88911-964-3

Understanding Innovation in Canadian Industry, Fred Gault (ed.), 2003
Paper ISBN 1-55339-030-X Cloth 1-55339-031-8

Delicate Dances: Public Policy and the Nonprofit Sector, Kathy L. Brock (ed.), 2003
Paper ISBN 0-88911-953-8 Cloth 0-88911-955-4

Beyond the National Divide: Regional Dimensions of Industrial Relations, Mark
Thompson, Joseph B. Rose and Anthony E. Smith (eds.), 2003
Paper ISBN 0-88911-963-5 Cloth 0-88911-965-1

The Nonprofit Sector in Interesting Times: Case Studies in a Changing Sector, Kathy L.
Brock and Keith G. Banting (eds.), 2003
Paper ISBN 0-88911-941-4 Cloth 0-88911-943-0

Clusters Old and New: The Transition to a Knowledge Economy in Canada's Regions,
David A. Wolfe (ed.), 2003   Paper ISBN 0-88911-959-7 Cloth 0-88911-961-9

The e-Connected World: Risks and Opportunities, Stephen Coleman (ed.), 2003
Paper ISBN 0-88911-945-7 Cloth 0-88911-947-3

Knowledge Clusters and Regional Innovation: Economic Development in Canada,
J. Adam Holbrook and David A. Wolfe (eds.), 2002
Paper ISBN 0-88911-919-8 Cloth 0-88911-917-1

Lessons of Everyday Law/Le droit du quotidien, Roderick Alexander Macdonald, 2002
Paper ISBN 0-88911-915-5 Cloth 0-88911-913-9

*Improving Connections Between Governments and Nonprofit and Voluntary
Organizations: Public Policy and the Third Sector*, Kathy L. Brock (ed.), 2002
Paper ISBN 0-88911-899-X Cloth 0-88911-907-4

Centre for the Study of Democracy

*The Authentic Voice of Canada: R.B. Bennett's Speeches in the House of Lords, 1941-
1947*, Christopher McCreery and Arthur Milnes (eds.), 2009. Paper 978-1-55339-275-0
Cloth ISBN 978-1-55339-276-7

*In Roosevelt's Bright Shadow: Presidential Addresses About Canada from Taft to Obama
in Honour of FDR's 1938 Speech at Queen's University*, Arthur Milnes (ed.), 2009
Paper ISBN 978-1-55339-230-9 Cloth ISBN 978-1-55339-231-6

*Politics of Purpose, 40th Anniversary Edition, The Right Honourable John N. Turner
17th Prime Minister of Canada*, Elizabeth McIninch and Arthur Milnes (eds.),
2009   Paper ISBN 978-1-55339-227-9 Cloth ISBN 978-1-55339-224-8

*Bridging the Divide: Religious Dialogue and Universal Ethics, Papers for
The InterAction Council*, Thomas S. Axworthy (ed.), 2008
Paper ISBN 978-1-55339-219-4 Cloth ISBN 978-1-55339-220-0

Institute of Intergovernmental Relations

The Democratic Dilemma: Reforming the Canadian Senate, Jennifer Smith (ed.), 2009.
Paper 978-1-55339-190-6

Canada: The State of the Federation 2006/07: Transitions – Fiscal and Political Federalism in an Era of Change, vol. 20, John R. Allan, Thomas J. Courchene, and Christian Leuprecht (eds.), 2009
Paper ISBN 978-1-55339-189-0 Cloth ISBN 978-1-55339-191-3

Comparing Federal Systems, Third Edition, Ronald L. Watts, 2008
Paper ISBN 978-1-55339-188-3

Canada: The State of the Federation 2005: Quebec and Canada in the New Century – New Dynamics, New Opportunities, vol. 19, Michael Murphy (ed.), 2007
Paper ISBN 978-1-55339-018-3 Cloth ISBN 978-1-55339-017-6

Spheres of Governance: Comparative Studies of Cities in Multilevel Governance Systems, Harvey Lazar and Christian Leuprecht (eds.), 2007
Paper ISBN 978-1-55339-019-0 Cloth ISBN 978-1-55339-129-6

Canada: The State of the Federation 2004, vol. 18, Municipal-Federal-Provincial Relations in Canada, Robert Young and Christian Leuprecht (eds.), 2006
Paper ISBN 1-55339-015-6 Cloth ISBN 1-55339-016-4

Canadian Fiscal Arrangements: What Works, What Might Work Better, Harvey Lazar (ed.), 2005 Paper ISBN 1-55339-012-1 Cloth ISBN 1-55339-013-X

Canada: The State of the Federation 2003, vol. 17, Reconfiguring Aboriginal-State Relations, Michael Murphy (ed.), 2005
Paper ISBN 1-55339-010-5 Cloth ISBN 1-55339-011-3

Canada: The State of the Federation 2002, vol. 16, Reconsidering the Institutions of Canadian Federalism, J. Peter Meekison, Hamish Telford and Harvey Lazar (eds.), 2004 Paper ISBN 1-55339-009-1 Cloth ISBN 1-55339-008-3

Federalism and Labour Market Policy: Comparing Different Governance and Employment Strategies, Alain Noël (ed.), 2004
Paper ISBN 1-55339-006-7 Cloth ISBN 1-55339-007-5

The Impact of Global and Regional Integration on Federal Systems: A Comparative Analysis, Harvey Lazar, Hamish Telford and Ronald L. Watts (eds.), 2003
Paper ISBN 1-55339-002-4 Cloth ISBN 1-55339-003-2

Canada: The State of the Federation 2001, vol. 15, Canadian Political Culture(s) in Transition, Hamish Telford and Harvey Lazar (eds.), 2002
Paper ISBN 0-88911-863-9 Cloth ISBN 0-88911-851-5

Federalism, Democracy and Disability Policy in Canada, Alan Puttee (ed.), 2002
Paper ISBN 0-88911-855-8 Cloth ISBN 1-55339-001-6, ISBN 0-88911-845-0 (set)

Comparaison des régimes fédéraux, 2e éd., Ronald L. Watts, 2002
Paper ISBN 1-55339-005-9

John Deutsch Institute for the Study of Economic Policy